NANA'S
CREOLE ITALIAN TABLE

The
SOUTHERN TABLE

Cynthia LeJeune Nobles
Series Editor

ELIZABETH M. WILLIAMS

NANA'S CREOLE ITALIAN TABLE

Recipes and Stories from
**SICILIAN
NEW ORLEANS**

LOUISIANA STATE UNIVERSITY PRESS

BATON ROUGE

Published with the assistance of the V. Ray Cardozier Fund

Published by Louisiana State University Press
lsupress.org

Manufactured in the United States of America
First printing

DESIGNER: Mandy McDonald Scallan
TYPEFACES: Chaparral Pro, text; Brandon Printed One, display
PRINTER AND BINDER: Sheridan Books, Inc.

All family photographs are from the author's personal collection.

Cover image: Goskova Tatiana/Shutterstock

Library of Congress Cataloging-in-Publication Data
Names: Williams, Elizabeth M. (Elizabeth Marie), author.
Title: Nana's Creole Italian table : recipes and stories from Sicilian New
    Orleans / Elizabeth M. Williams.
Description: Baton Rouge : Louisiana State University Press, 2022. |
    Includes index.
Identifiers: LCCN 2021034306 | ISBN 9780807177136 (cloth)
Subjects: LCSH: Cooking, Italian—Sicilian style. | Cooking, Creole. |
    Cooking—Louisiana—New Orleans. | Sicilian
    Americans—Food—Louisiana—New Orleans. | LCGFT: Cookbooks.
Classification: LCC TX723.2.S55 W55 2022 | DDC 641.59458—dc23
LC record available at https://lccn.loc.gov/2021034306

To Eric, Mark, Olivia, and Isabella

🍴🍴🍴🍴

CONTENTS

ACKNOWLEDGMENTS

Thank goodness that cuisine is a social invention. It develops little by little in people's kitchens and at their tables. I cannot express enough times how much I owe to my Nana, my mother, and those people who let me into their kitchens and invited me to their tables. Without their generosity of spirit I would not have been able to write this book or cook any of these dishes. And I would not have had the pleasure of tasting the wonderful meals and dishes they made for me and with me. And I would not have learned so much about life and living.

And thanks to my editors, Cindy Nobles, Susan A. Murray, and Catherine Kadair, who make my writing better and keep me honest. And thanks to LSU Press for giving me a platform.

NANA'S
CREOLE ITALIAN TABLE

INTRODUCTION

At first glance, you might think this is a book about my Sicilian-born grandmother, my Nana, and her culinary acolyte, my grandfather, Papa, who was born in New Orleans, but whose parents came from Sicily. It is a book somewhat about my mother, who cooked our family meals with the Sicilian cooking rules she learned from her mother, but did so in the New Orleans atmosphere of gumbo and jambalaya. It is a book a bit less about me, because I grew up in a home of Italian comfort food, but one that included my decidedly not-Sicilian father, Cleve Williams, a New Orleanian who was a fan of pimento cheese and pickled pork and who, if given a choice, would take rice over pasta. This book is hardly at all about my children and grandchildren; rather, it is for them. Their generations can only look back over their shoulders to Sicily as merely a foggy impression that is largely myth.

When you look closer, you'll see that this book is about the thousands of Sicilians who settled in New Orleans in the nineteenth and early twentieth centuries. Most of these hardy folks came here with nothing but ended up making their marks on the city in music, business, politics, and food. Through my family's stories I focus on the food, but I also explore Sicilian identity and culture. This book, then, is part memoir, part history, and part cookbook. It is indirectly a roadmap to New Orleans's Sicilian immigration and its ultimate Creolization as seen through the eyes of my ancestors.

I grew up in and now live in New Orleans, where we certainly eat traditional American Italian food. But we also wholly embrace a cuisine known as "Creole Italian," which is the culinary intermingling of peasant-style Sicilian with relatively refined French Creole. The Sicilians who sailed to New Orleans more than a hundred years ago—my grandmother being one of them—initiated this hybrid way of cooking. This is the food I grew up on, the product of a culinary transformation that impacted everyone in the city, from French and African Creoles to immigrant Germans and Irish. But the recipes from my grandparents are more than the marriage of strong traditional Creole and Sicilian cooking. They tie into the larger story about cultural transformation and the weakening of the cord that binds subsequent generations.

I witnessed my family transition from being immigrants to America to becoming indistinguishable from all other Americans and New Orleanians. The immigration process is never easy. But the stress of moving to a new environment is reduced when many immigrants from the same location settle in the same place at the same time, just as the twenty thousand or so Sicilian immigrants did around the turn of the twentieth century in New Orleans. Arriving together and living in close proximity, they helped each other become members of their new communities and also helped preserve their old culture, at least in the first few generations. I was fortunate enough to be able to live a part of my life in that Sicilian community, as well as enjoy the privileges of being born in New Orleans.

Around the 1880s, it was the city's need for cheap labor that lured Sicilian immigrants to New Orleans, and they came en masse. My family's personal story, as well as the stories of the thousands of New Orleanians of Sicilian descent, is, of course, unique. In general, Italian acculturation in this city was ardent and sometimes met with resistance from Americans and Italians alike. But this immigrant saga, like most others, ultimately blossomed into a rich cultural exchange. Though my family's observance of Sicilian culture and traditions has weakened through the generations, the influence of those traditions has left its mark on the city of New Orleans, particularly in its food.

One of the most visible manifestations of any immigrant evolution is what is served on family tables. When there are massive numbers of immigrants, this also happens at the city's collective table. No matter an immigrant's country of origin, food plays an important role in making their new home feel like home. The transformation of immigrant food into something completely American is a metaphor for the Americanization of any immigrant. It is an important element of our incredible melting pot, and the incorporation of immigrant cuisines into a host country's food culture includes progressive bumps in the road: the food and its people are first viewed as problematic; the food is then viewed with suspicion as different, even threatening; and, finally, the food becomes trendy, eventually passing into ordinary.

The dishes my Sicilian ancestors brought here are now hardly recognizable as Italian. Many shapes and sizes of original dishes have taken on new proportions. Take that very American meatball. Too big to be a real Italian meatball, it has found its way into a po'boy slathered with Creole red gravy and traditionally dressed New Orleans style, with mayonnaise, shredded lettuce, sliced tomatoes, and pickles. We are extremely aware that such fare is neither Italian nor generally American; it is the food of New Orleans. (Don't be fooled into thinking that it is a meatball sub or hoagie.)

Meatball po'boys have become a New Orleans mainstay, and our city would not be the same without a few other popular Sicilian culinary contributions, such as the snoball, the muffuletta, and the stuffed artichoke. When I was younger, in addition to regularly enjoying these iconic treats, I tasted some real Italian versions of foods my grandmother and my mother fixed when they were feeling particularly nostalgic, foods such as fried herbs, the chickpea fritter known as *panelle,* and *agliata,* an Italian version of mayonnaise. I was fortunate enough to watch my relatives prepare those and many other esoteric dishes, and I have included recipes for many of them in this book.

Italian immigration on the whole has certainly left its mark on the way America eats. When transplanted to our various states and regions, Italian food made many adaptations, and these tweaked dishes have truly become American food. Specifically, how did this happen? When my grandmother served her family something familiar, she not only nourished, but she mitigated the longing for home and the frustrations and difficulties of adapting to a new culture and language. But in new surroundings, traditional dishes often change, mostly because crucial ingredients can be impossible to find. There's also the temptation of using newfound spices and seasonings, and there's the influence of the cooking styles of new neighbors. My Nana, for example, found comfort in making her Sunday red gravy, the New Orleans version of marinara. But I often wonder if she realized how much Creole south Louisiana's reliance on roux, onion, celery, and bell pepper had influenced what went into that pot.

The younger generations of New Orleans's original Sicilians are now spread far and wide, and hopefully they're taking their knowledge and love of Creole Italian food along with them. Back here in New Orleans, we're simmering shrimp in red gravy, grilling oysters in butter and garlic, and stuffing whole artichokes with seasoned breadcrumbs. We're also stewing whole beef roasts in tomato sauce, and we're floating boiled eggs in our gumbo. To the average American these dishes might sound foreign, but they were all invented here; they're all part of Creole Italian cuisine.

Unlike me, my children and grandchildren did not grow up in a Sicilian community and so lack a close connection to their Sicilian heritage. As time goes on, maybe my children, grandchildren, and my grandchildren's children will make their own version of American culture. I hope that these recipes and remembrances strike a chord with them and with those of you of Sicilian or Italian descent. I hope my family can use this written word as a record of their past, but I also hope that they will look to the future. This book is not about holding onto what has been but, rather, about knowing it. And I hope that we can see how we all, no matter who we are, change from generation to generation, as food and culture carry us through the years. *Mangia bene.*

ADAPTING

Few members of my family make a Creole Italian recipe the same way. When I was growing up, it was common to eat diverse recipe interpretations, because all of my aunts and my mother and grandmother liked different things. So, in this book I sometimes include a couple of ways of cooking the same thing. These comparisons give a better visual of the transformation of Sicilian foods to uniquely American ones. These recipes are the result of a culinary metamorphosis that began well over a hundred years ago, when Sicilians flocked to New Orleans and left their stamp on the way we eat. I include the following three recipes in the introduction because they starkly demonstrate how immigrant recipes change, both within the family and in the culture. I call the first recipe Three-Generation Olive Salad because, though it's my version, it is basically the way my mother made this salad from a recipe she modified from my grandmother's. For my part, I wanted to add freshness to my mother's recipe, so I include thinly sliced fennel and baby artichokes, which add crunch. These two ingredients also cut the saltiness.

THREE-GENERATION OLIVE SALAD

MAKES ABOUT 2 QUARTS

Olive salad is essential on a traditional muffuletta sandwich. This salad also tastes wonderful on an antipasto platter, in a tossed green salad, stuffed in fresh Creole tomatoes, and layered Napoleon-style between slices of tomato.

Old New Orleans was familiar with olives, of course. The early Creoles even used broken green and black olives to make tapenade. But it was the Sicilians who frugally mixed broken olives, both green and black, into a salad, not a paste. To stretch the salad, they added finely chopped vegetables.

As in any recipe, the better the ingredients, the greater your chance of success. In this particular case, the better the olives, the better the salad. Unless you are desperate, this does not mean buying something in a can labeled "chopped black olives." The dish will taste infinitely better if you purchase properly cured black and green olives and chop them yourself.

1. In a large bowl, mash the anchovy with 1 tablespoon of the olive oil until the anchovy totally dissolves. If you think you need more olive oil, add another tablespoon. Mix in all other ingredients except the remaining olive oil and the basil leaves.

2. Add enough olive oil to barely cover the mixture. Stir well so that everything is evenly distributed. Let it sit an hour, then taste. If it needs more acidity, add a bit more lemon juice. Because of the olives and anchovy, this salad will probably not need additional salt, but add it if you like. If you want, throw in fresh basil leaves right before serving.

1 anchovy filet

About 1½ cups fruity olive oil

About 10 boiled and quartered baby artichokes (Fresh is best, but if you use frozen, that's about 2 packs, boiled and cooled. In a pinch, canned can be substituted, but the taste and texture will be inferior.)

3 cups coarsely chopped cured green olives with pimento

2 cups coarsely chopped black olives

1 cup finely diced celery

1 cup finely diced raw carrot

1 cup finely diced raw cauliflower (optional)

1 very, very thinly sliced lemon, including any juice you can save

1 fennel bulb sliced thinly on a mandoline

4 garlic cloves, minced

6 tablespoons chopped fresh oregano, or 4 tablespoons dried

¼ cup coarsely chopped capers

Freshly ground black pepper, to taste

Salt (optional)

1 cup fresh basil leaves (optional)

JOSEPHINE'S OLIVE SALAD

MAKES ABOUT 2 QUARTS

My mother, Josephine, added the thinly sliced lemons, a much-needed zing of acid that I think makes this dish more interesting. As the lemons age in the salad, you can eat the entire lemon, peel and all.

1. In a large bowl, mash the anchovy with 1 tablespoon of the olive oil until the anchovy totally dissolves. If you need more olive oil, add another tablespoon. Mix in the rest of the ingredients, except for the remaining olive oil.

2. Add enough olive oil to barely cover the mixture. Stir well so that everything is evenly distributed. Let it sit an hour, then taste. If it needs more acidity add a bit more lemon juice. Because of the olives and anchovy, this salad will probably not need additional salt, but add it if you like. Garnish with freshly cracked black pepper.

1 anchovy filet

About 1½ cups fruity olive oil

3 cups coarsely chopped cured green olives with pimento

2 cups coarsely chopped black olives

1 cup finely diced celery

1 cup finely diced raw carrot

1 cup finely diced raw cauliflower

1 lemon sliced as thinly as possible

4 cloves garlic minced

6 tablespoons chopped fresh oregano or 4 tablespoons dried oregano

¼ cup capers, coarsely chopped

¼ cup lemon juice

Salt (optional)

For serving: freshly cracked black pepper

NANA'S OLIVE SALAD

MAKES ABOUT 2 QUARTS

This is my Nana's version of olive salad. It is extremely similar to the original salty, chopped olive, garlic, and vegetable condiment that was sold by New Orleans's various Sicilian grocers and slathered on muffulettas.

1. In a large bowl, mash the anchovy with 1 tablespoon of the olive oil until the anchovy totally dissolves. If you need more olive oil, add another tablespoon. Mix in all other ingredients except the black pepper.

2. Add enough olive oil to just barely cover the mixture. Stir well so that everything is evenly distributed. Let it sit an hour, then taste. If it needs more acidity, add a bit more lemon juice. Because of the olives and anchovy, this salad will probably not need additional salt, but add it if you like. Garnish with freshly cracked black pepper.

1 anchovy filet

About 1½ cups fruity olive oil

3 cups coarsely chopped cured green olives with pimento

2 cups coarsely chopped black olives

1 cup finely diced celery

1 cup finely diced raw carrot

1 cup finely diced raw cauliflower

4 cloves garlic minced

6 tablespoons chopped fresh oregano or 4 tablespoons dried oregano

¼ cup coarsely chopped capers

¼ cup freshly squeezed lemon juice

Salt (optional)

For serving: freshly ground black pepper

CHAPTER 1

COMING TO NEW ORLEANS
Condiments and Snacks

Unni mancianu dui, mancianau tri. (There is always room for one more.)
—Sicilian proverb

I want my children and my grandchildren to have an awareness of their connection to the Sicilians who came to America and laid a foundation for their lives. These immigrants did not intend to change New Orleans, but their sheer numbers made their influence inevitable. And because they migrated to a food-crazy city and they were from Sicily, eating and food culture became a natural area of confluence.

With all the talk today about illegal and legal immigration, my imagination goes back to my maternal grandmother and her parents and their journey—leaving Palermo, Sicily, together to make a new life in New Orleans. They spoke no English. But they chose New Orleans because it was known as a Sicilian haven, with many of their countrymen already having made this city their home.

Almost from its European beginning, New Orleans has been home to Sicilian immigrants. In particular, after the Civil War thousands came to Louisiana to work in the sugarcane fields. Yet another and even bigger wave came to New Orleans at the turn of the twentieth century. Each boatload of Sicilians brought along their food culture, and over the generations they influenced the food of New Orleans, even as they intermarried with other New Orleanians, moved all over the Greater New Orleans area, and became part of the city's culture.

On May 12, 1910, my Nana—my maternal grandmother, Elisabetta Lecce—came to New Orleans at the age of eighteen, on the SS *Liguria*. She was the oldest of nine children, and on the voyage she helped her parents take care of her younger siblings. Her immigra-

My grandmother, Nana, as a young woman

nose; and she was plump, with black curly hair that gradually grayed throughout her life. Not only was she a great cook, but she had a lovely singing voice, and she was a member of the New Orleans Italian Opera Company, an all-amateur troupe. She could sing in many languages, and she sang around the house while she worked. I loved listening to her sing. And it was through singing that my Nana and her parents and siblings became enmeshed in New Orleans's larger community of Sicilians.

My mother, Josephine, also cooked well, but she did not have the same gift for cooking as her mother, or for singing. It was a big family disappointment that my mother could not carry a tune; somehow, she could not hear herself sing. Everyone would laugh in frustration as she would try to teach me songs, which I would sing the way she did, and the tune was always wrong. Mother said that she'd been required to take choir in school and that she would be asked to only mouth the words because she was so off, unlike her mother, a sassy singer with a strong mezzo-soprano voice.

When I knew her, my Nana couldn't move well because of rheumatoid arthritis, but that sauciness of Carmen and the other mezzo roles she knew came out gracefully when she sang. I can only imagine how her tiny body—she was less than 5 feet tall—would taunt her tenor when she was young. We all knew that we were growing up when we became taller than Nana. Despite all evidence, at every measuring she'd insist that we were not taller than her. But throughout her life her breathtaking voice was bigger than all of us.

GRATING BREADCRUMBS

The values the Lecce family brought here were love of family, joy of life, willingness to work hard, and frugality. Thrift was a way of life for my Nana. She made

tion entry record shows that when she arrived in the Port of New Orleans she was described as a servant. My great-grandfather, Giuseppe Lecce, whom I never knew, was a butcher by trade. After arriving in New Orleans, he worked in the French Market. Two of my grandmother's three brothers were also butchers. The youngest brother, Joseph, worked with my parents in our family freight-forwarding business.

My Nana had olive skin, black eyes, and a Roman

her own breadcrumbs by grating stale braided Italian loaves on a box grater.

The bread for the crumbs came from loaves that had been sitting around a few days. When she was younger, Nana often baked her own bread, but by the time I was in high school, she bought it. Sometimes she bought bread from United Bakery on St. Bernard Avenue. United was renowned for its Italian breads, especially round, seeded muffuletta loaves, which they provided to Central Grocery and Progressive Grocery for their famous muffuletta sandwiches. United also baked a hard-crusted braided bread that would stand up to any sauce.

When I visited Nana I was often given small jobs, and one of them was grating breadcrumbs. I learned the hard way to keep my knuckles away from the box's raised, sharpened holes. My Aunt Jerry's husband, my Uncle Buster, had made Nana a special grater and breadcrumb holder. The base was a wooden box about the size of a thick phone book. He hinged the base on one of the short sides so that it could swing open, making it easy to remove the breadcrumbs that fell inside. He made the grating part with a piece of sheet metal that he punctured in close rows with huge nails. The pierced metal pieces opened into sharp petals on the working side. This cheap, clever invention was great for grating and capturing breadcrumbs.

Both my Nana and her sister Jerry—actually my great-aunt, but I always called her Aunt Jerry—seasoned those breadcrumbs with grated cheese, dried oregano, dried parsley, and dried basil. Each Sicilian cook seemed to have their own version of seasoned breadcrumbs, and each version reflected the family's taste.

Today, it would probably be hard to find the culinary tradition of making your own breadcrumbs. Even in my childhood that practice of bread frugality was changing. With our busy lives and the wide availability of cheap bread, the Sicilian community I grew up in began to make stuffed artichokes with Progresso-brand breadcrumbs instead of making our own. We bought Progresso because it was a New Orleans company founded by fellow Sicilians.

Actually, every home cook I knew used the same store-bought products to make our traditional dishes. The result was that our food during the 1960s and 1970s grew much more uniform in taste and appearance. I think my grandmother and my mother were some of the last holdouts. My mother was too frugal (some would say too cheap) to buy breadcrumbs. "Why," she'd ask, "when you can make them?" Mom also felt that her breadcrumbs tasted better than whatever came in a cardboard tube.

The Progresso line of convenience products, now owned by General Mills, was born of the Americanization of Sicilian culture in New Orleans. By the 1960s, most of America was turning to prepackaged foods for ease and time-savings, and I knew very few who were immune to the allure of convenience. Through the use of foods such as grocery-bought breadcrumbs, Sicilians further assimilated into the mainstream. With everyone using the same breadcrumbs, recipes were standardized, and this made our dishes more attractive and accessible to non-Sicilians.

Nana never worked in the food industry in New Orleans, although she was peripherally part of it. (If she had, maybe her English would have lost its heavy accent.) In her own way she was a transmitter of the emerging food culture: that curious combination of New Orleans and Sicily. Specifically, she had a terrific palate and could duplicate anything she tasted, whether it was served at someone's home or in a restaurant. She and I often tasted her cooking together. We would sit at her kitchen table, and she made sure I had a forkful of everything. There were never any exceptions.

Fortunately for me, Nana was never shy or withholding about sharing her food wisdom. When I was about eight years old, someone who had been invited to dinner brought Nana a bottle of really sweet wine. I'm not sure what it was, but it was not Marsala, which Nana was certainly familiar with, since she regularly drank sweet Marsala with cookies and candied citrus peel. I visited Nana the day after she hosted her dinner, and that's when she opened the bottle. She put two thimbles full of wine in two small glasses. In my glass she added a little water. Her glass, she filled. She then pulled two biscotti out of a tin—one for each of us. I watched as she dipped her biscotto into her glass. I followed suit. I took a bite. The wine tasted sweet but also a bit sour. (Looking back on it, it was probably cheap wine that had been sweetened to make it palatable.) As we each took a sip of our wine, I felt as though I was sharing so much with my grandmother and learning life's lessons. She explained to me that the wine was too sweet to drink without a biscotto, and that one day I would appreciate knowing such a thing. "Marsala would be better," she explained. This was mysterious advice, but I never forgot it.

A WALKING SALAD DRESSING

Olive oil is a highly important flavor in Sicilian cooking, certainly more essential than butter. It is often added at the end of cooking as a garnish, used as a base for salad dressings, and used to flavor pasta. For cooking, however, a pomace oil or other neutral oil was commonly used because so much of the olive flavor is lost when the oil is heated.

Olive oil had other uses. When I was young, my grandmother used olive oil as a hair conditioner. And when she babysat me and my younger brother, the lotion for his diaper changes and post bath was extra-virgin olive oil. My brother smelled good enough to eat. I can only assume that as a baby I, too, smelled like olive oil. My mother didn't use olive oil on us; she used commercial baby oil. She thought that a baby smelling like olive oil was over-the-top, as she bridged the gap of being an American of Sicilian heritage.

As I got older and she became more American, my Nana bought scented hand cream and commercially made hair conditioners. That, however, was a purely economic decision. Hand lotion and hair conditioner were cheaper than olive oil.

When my two children had cradle cap, I'd go straight to olive oil to get rid of it. And it worked wonders. Remembering the scents of my childhood, I did try to apply the oil before a bath so that my sons didn't always smell like olive oil.

As an older child, I didn't smell like olive oil. Instead, I smelled like garlic. One thing my grandmother insisted on was my daily clove of garlic. Raw. When I trotted down the street to her home every day, I was always rewarded with a clove of garlic. This was not to ward off vampires, although I am sure it could have, but to keep me healthy. This was my Nana's version of a daily vitamin pill. I was seldom sick, so I guess it worked. I don't remember when Nana stopped making us eat garlic. What I do know is that I must have spent some part of my childhood smelling like salad.

ARANCINI

During the twentieth century so many Sicilians in New Orleans lived in the French Quarter, the Little Palermo, that they eventually spilled out into the neighboring faubourg (neighborhood) known as Tremé. My great-grandparents and my grandparents lived in Tremé, where there was a mixing of Sicilians and the African Americans who originally lived there. Associating with these new neighbors meant that Sicilians came into contact with calas, dessert-like fried rice fritters. Unlike sweet calas, arancini are savory, but they are still made of rice and represent another example of frugality, like calas. Both African Americans and Sicilians were making something delicious from the leftovers of one of Louisiana's top agricultural crops.

2 cups water

1 teaspoon salt

1 cup raw rice

1 cup shredded mozzarella

2 tablespoons pine nuts

2 tablespoons chopped parsley

2 large eggs, beaten

2 cups Seasoned Breadcrumbs (recipe page 101 or purchased), divided

Vegetable oil for frying

1. In a medium saucepan, bring the water and salt to a boil and stir in the rice. Bring back to a boil, lower to a simmer, cover, and cook until rice has absorbed all the water and is tender, 20 to 25 minutes. Remove from heat and cool.

2. Mix cheese, pine nuts, and parsley together in a bowl. Set aside.

3. Mix the cooled rice, beaten eggs, and all but ¼ cup of the breadcrumbs together in a large bowl. When the ingredients are thoroughly mixed, scoop out ¼ cup and roll into balls. With your thumb, make a deep indentation in the center of each ball. Place a teaspoon of the cheese mixture in the indentation. Bring the rice mixture over the cheese to remake a ball. Roll the balls in the remaining breadcrumbs. Refrigerate an hour.

4. Heat 1 inch oil in a heavy skillet to 350°F. Fry the rice balls until golden and crispy all over. This should take about 4 minutes. Drain on paper towels. Serve warm as a snack or a light meal.

CAPONATA

Even though my Papa had a terrific garden, he really only grew enough produce for household eating. Any extra was traded with neighbors. (The exception was three pear trees, which produced an enormous crop, and he usually ended up giving most of that away.) But a cousin from my Papa's brother's family lived in Amite, and he had a proper farm. His was a traditional truck-farming family that brought their harvests into the city to sell. And because we were family, they often gave us their excess of eggplants, tomatoes, and onions.

When that gift of vegetables arrived, my mother and I would make a huge batch of caponata that we preserved in glass jars and ate all year. Processing caponata jars in a water bath was one of my favorite things to do with my mother. We'd begin by chopping vegetables and sautéing them, making the whole kitchen smell wonderful. Every time we opened a jar, those wonderful aromas took us back to the day we made it.

This is a quick-and-dirty caponata that tastes really good, even though it lacks the complexity of a traditional caponata from Sicily. The sweet undertone of this caponata is produced by using sweet pickles. The ingredient proportions listed can easily be expanded, and they depend on the size of your eggplant.

½–¾ cup olive oil

5 cups cubed eggplant (about one large eggplant), unpeeled

1½ cups very roughly chopped onions

1 cup roughly chopped celery

½ cup chopped carrots, in ½-inch cubes

3 cloves garlic, minced

One large can (10–12 ounces) whole plum tomatoes, with liquid

2 tablespoons capers (optional)

2 tablespoons pine nuts (optional, not everyone uses them)

Dried oregano (optional–I use it, but it is not traditional.)

2 tablespoons wine vinegar

Half a lemon, seeded and chopped

1 or 2 bay leaves

1 teaspoon salt

1 teaspoon ground black pepper

Sugar (optional)

Finely chopped sweet pickle (optional, if you want a sweet flavor)

1. In a large skillet, heat the olive oil over medium heat. Sauté the eggplant and remove after it browns. This might require a few batches. In the same skillet, cook onions, celery, carrots, and garlic until onion is just tender, about 6 minutes. Remove all vegetables.

2. Reserve the liquid from the can of tomatoes and crush the tomatoes in your hands. Add them to the skillet. Cook the tomatoes, stirring occasionally, and let it caramelize and sweeten, about 15 minutes. Add the cooked vegetables and the tomato liquid. If you're using capers, pine nuts, and oregano, now's the time to add them.

3. Add the wine vinegar, lemon, and bay leaves. After it all comes to a simmer, cook uncovered at least 20 minutes, stirring frequently. The mixture should be the texture of a thick stew. Add salt and pepper. Taste and decide whether to add sugar and chopped pickle. Remove bay leaves and let cool to room temperature. Refrigerate overnight and let come back to room temperature before serving.

CAPONATA 2

MAKES ABOUT A GALLON

This is the richer and more complex version of caponata. It is worth the time it takes to make it.

1. Heat half the olive oil over medium heat in a large pot. Add the tomato paste and cook, stirring constantly, for 2 minutes. Add the raisins and stir. Add the eggplant and cook until soft, about 10 minutes. Remove from the pot.

2. Add the onions, adding a bit more oil if needed, and cook until the onions soften and become golden, about 8 minutes. Remove the onions from the pot. Add the celery and cook until tender, about 8 minutes. Add the remainder of the oil and return the eggplant, onions, and celery to the pot. Add the bell pepper and cook 2 minutes. Add the tomatoes, carrot, and garlic and cook 8 minutes. Add the black and green olives, capers, bay leaves, and cinnamon. Stir well and then cook uncovered 20 minutes.

3. Add the wine vinegar. Cook and reduce the liquid 10 minutes. The vegetables should be soft. Taste for salt. (The capers and the olives add salt, so you will have to adjust at this point.) Add the pepper, then refrigerate overnight. Serve at room temperature, garnished with fresh basil leaves and pine nuts.

½ cup olive oil, divided

1 tablespoon tomato paste

3 tablespoons minced raisins

2¼ pounds eggplant, unpeeled and diced

1 pound onions, roughly chopped

1¼ pounds celery stalks, chopped into a large dice

1 red bell pepper, coarsely chopped

1⅔ pounds fresh tomatoes, roughly chopped

1 carrot, grated

3 cloves garlic, minced

½ pound pitted black olives, roughly chopped

½ pound pitted green olives, roughly chopped

6 ounces salted capers, chopped and rinsed well

2 bay leaves

Pinch of cinnamon

⅓ cup wine vinegar

Fine sea salt

Freshly ground black pepper

For serving: fresh basil leaves and pine nuts

GREMOLATA

MAKES ABOUT 1 CUP

Gremolata is the citrusy all-purpose seasoning relish that tastes like Italy. Unlike a French mirepoix, it is intended to be served raw. The traditional ingredients are lemon and orange zests, parsley, and garlic, which meld together to create a fresh taste that gives a final zing to long-cooked soups and sauces. Gremolata is also delicious on grilled or broiled meats, rather like a chimichurri.

This recipe is forgiving. Use what you have on hand, even a grapefruit, and just about any kind of fresh herb. I use a mini-processor to make gremolata. My Nana would grate her citrus and placed it on a cutting board. She then mashed peeled garlic cloves with the side of a knife and added them to the citrus zest. Her last step was to add a pile of just-minced herbs, minced with her mezzaluna (a curved, rocking knife), and mix everything together. Her herbs came from my Papa's lovely garden, where he grew parsley, oregano, and basil.

In the interest of channeling the spirit of frugality, after you have zested your lemons and oranges for gremolata, remember to eat the pulp and juice. In my childhood home there was always denuded citrus in the refrigerator, and those fruits did eventually get used. In the same spirit, use the stems of your herbs in gremolata—not the woody stems, but those that are tender and fresh. If some herb parts are too woody and stringy, put them in the freezer and use to make stock.

1 cup of tightly packed parsley (can be a mixture of any green herbs, but should be at least half parsley)

Zest of 1 lemon

Zest of half an orange

3 cloves garlic

Place all ingredients on a cutting board and chop together until the mixture is fine. If you have a mini–food processor you can use that. Parsley stems are full of flavor, so in my house we chop parsley stems down to at least the middle. The soft stems of oregano and basil are also usable.

FRIED HERBS

MAKES AS MANY AS YOU WANT

Nana enjoyed eating and preparing good food, and when working in the kitchen she was not a shortcut artist. She did everything in the manner she had been taught, which meant cooking totally from scratch. Sitting around her table we learned that eating this wonderful food with each other was its own pleasure. It also pleased her to watch us enjoy her cooking, which often included extra little things, such as fried herbs.

Like gremolata, fried herbs add a fresh note to a long-cooked dish. The beauty of frying herbs is that as they are cooked, they soften and take on a mild earthy flavor. Fresh oregano and woody herbs like rosemary, for example, are strong, often strong enough to overpower. But when they're fried, the flavors mellow out, allowing you to use these herbs in large quantities as an ingredient in a dish. For a garnish, Nana fried soft herbs like oregano and sage. These same fried herbs could also be chopped and added to a dish for seasoning.

Wash and dry the herbs. The leaves must be completely dry before frying. Heat 1 inch of olive oil in a small skillet over medium heat. When you can put your open hand above the oil and feel the heat, add a leaf. If it crumples, the oil is too hot. Add leaves only a few at a time so that you can attend to them. It takes less than a minute for them to crisp. Drain on a paper towel.

*Rosemary should be rubbed with a paper towel to remove dirt. Do not wash rosemary with water; it is impossible to dry the wet sprigs. Only cook with rosemary's tender new tips, and cut those tips into sprigs about 1 or 2 inches long, depending on whether you're using them as garnish or as an ingredient. It takes about a minute to fry a rosemary sprig.

Fresh herbs, such as sage leaves or whole sprigs of oregano, parsley, and rosemary*

Olive oil for frying

OLIVE OIL AND LEMON SPREAD

MAKES ABOUT A CUP

If you find mayonnaise rich but bland, try this instead. The pectin in the lemon (or other citrus) skin will emulsify the oil, so you don't need egg. In Nana's day, lemons were abundant, and this was what she typically used instead of mayonnaise. I like it on freshly sliced tomatoes and sandwiches.

1 lemon (or 5 or 6 kumquats)

1 cup olive oil

Salt and pepper to taste

1. Wash the lemon and quarter it. (Don't worry about the seeds, they'll emulsify.) Place the lemon quarters into a blender. Add half of the oil, as well as the salt and pepper.

2. Slowly start the blender and gradually raise the speed until the oil and lemon are emulsified. Drizzle the rest of the oil into the blender while it is running.

3. Place the spread into a jar, cover with a lid, and refrigerate up to 3 weeks.

PANELLE (CHICKPEA FRIES)

MAKES 6 SERVINGS

Eating beans was essential in Sicily, where meat was not part of the daily diet. The poor learned to transform lowly chickpea flour into a treat, which was one of the magical things they did with what they had. When Sicilian immigrants came to New Orleans, meat did become something that could be part of their daily diet, but they also continued to eat culturally. This meant that *panelle* were often on the table.

2¾ cups chickpea flour

3 cups water

Peanut or canola oil for frying

Salt and pepper

1. In a large pot or saucepan thoroughly whisk together the chickpea flour and the water. Cook over medium heat to make a thick porridge, stirring constantly with a wooden spoon, about 6 minutes. Reduce heat to low. Stir and cook until the dough pulls away from the sides of the pan. Remove from heat.

2. For a traditional shape, use an offset spatula to spread portions of the mixture into several circles of about 5 to 7 inches in diameter. Keep the dough warm and pliable in the pan as you remove the batches. Allow the circles to cool and harden. Cut into wedges. (For a more French fry–like snack, pour the porridge onto a rimmed cookie pan and spread thinly and evenly. Allow to cool and harden. Cut with a sharp knife into strips resembling French fries.)

3. Heat 1 inch oil in a clean pot to 350°F. Fry the fritters in small batches until they float on the oil, turning at least once. Remove from the oil and drain on paper towels. Sprinkle with salt and pepper to taste.

PESTO

MAKES 2½ CUPS

Pesto provides a way to include a bit of protein (found in nuts) in the diet, and it adds a burst of flavor to most savory dishes. In Nana's day, pesto was also a good substitute for tomatoes when they weren't in season.

Tender herbs, such as parsley, go well with basil in this recipe. You can also simply use anything green, such as raw spinach, which makes a mild pesto. And consider trying different nuts.

Almost always, Nana's long-cooked dishes and soups were enhanced by the traditional spoonful of pesto added to each bowl, which was also a way to stretch the Parmagiano-Reggiano by not allowing each person to grate their own cheese. A tablespoon of pesto adds a lot of flavor to a bowl of soup, tossed on pasta, or spread on bruschetta. It's a great punch of flavor.

3 cups fresh basil leaves

4 garlic cloves

½ cup grated Parmagiano-Reggiano cheese or other hard Italian cheese, like Pecorino-Romano

⅓ cup pine nuts or almonds

½ teaspoon lemon zest

¾ cup extra-virgin olive oil

Salt to taste

Add the basil, garlic, cheese, nuts, and lemon zest to the bowl of a food processor. Begin to process the ingredients in the bowl, then slowly drizzle in the olive oil. Pesto should be smooth, but with a bit of texture. Adjust for salt. (Different cheeses have different salt levels, so taste before salting.)

PIMENTO CHEESE

Southerners love pimento cheese. My father was a big fan, and he bought jars of it from one of his favorite gas stations, which also sold pickled okra and pickled eggs. My Nana was appalled that anyone would eat pimentos from a can, so she developed this recipe for my father so that he wasn't relegated to eating inferior pimentos in his pimento cheese. Of course, she added Parmesan cheese to the mix, because what isn't better with Parmesan cheese? I like to serve it as a dip, and it's wonderful with celery sticks, on sandwiches, and on hot pasta.

1 pound Cheddar cheese, shredded

2 red bell peppers, roasted, seeded, and chopped

1 cup good mayonnaise

¼ cup grated Parmesan cheese

¼ cup Nana's Olive Salad (recipe page 6)

Salt and freshly ground black pepper to taste

Place all ingredients except salt and pepper in a large bowl and mix well, but gently. Taste for salt. (The mixture might be salty because of the olive salad and the cheese.) Add pepper to taste. Refrigerate until ready to serve.

NANA'S BASIC TOMATO SAUCE

MAKES ABOUT 2 QUARTS

This is my Nana's tomato sauce recipe. This sauce was so basic that we considered it a building block of most meals, so I've included it in the condiment chapter. There was always a pot of this sauce sitting on the stove, or at least that is how I remember it. Although this is the traditional Sicilian way of making tomato sauce, Nana condoned Creole red gravy, which calls for roux. Her attitude was much more tolerant than those of my great-aunts, who felt that red gravy was an abomination. They had nothing but disdain for the roux-based red stuff. Nana thought it worked on po'boys, just not on pasta. That is where she drew the line.

Nana also hated using sugar in tomato sauce, which is a common practice in south Louisiana. She thought sugar only added sweetness without adding depth of flavor. That is why she used grated carrots, which melt into the sauce, so their textural identity is lost. The natural sweetness of carrots adds a depth and complexity that sugar alone cannot. If you like your sauce sweeter, add another grated carrot.

I ate many a plate of pasta with this sauce. My Nana's tomato sauce is absolutely the best, and it is good on pasta, in lasagna, in chicken stew, simmered with a small roast, or over lots of delicious Italian sausage.

¼ cup extra-virgin olive oil

1 anchovy, mashed

3 large onions, finely chopped

5 cloves garlic, minced

2 carrots, grated

1 stalk celery, minced

1 small can (4 ounces) tomato paste

5 pounds tomatoes, put through a food mill or 3 (15-ounce) cans crushed Italian tomatoes

1 cup red wine

2 bay leaves, whole

2 tablespoons dried oregano

Zest and juice of half a lemon

Salt and pepper to taste

For serving: hot spaghetti and grated Parmigiano-Reggiano cheese

1. Heat oil over medium heat in a large pot with a heavy bottom. Slowly sauté anchovy until it dissolves. Sauté onions, garlic, carrots, and celery until soft. Add tomato paste and continue cooking until caramelized, about 15 minutes. Add the tomatoes, wine, and bay leaves. Stir. Cover and simmer at least an hour. (Cooking time for fresh tomatoes is longer.)

2. Continue simmering, uncovered, until thick. Add oregano, zest, and lemon juice. Cook 15 minutes. Serve tossed into spaghetti and topped with cheese.

NANA'S OLIVE SALAD *(page 6)*

CAPONATA *(page 12)*

ARANCINI *(page 11)*

NANA'S BASIC TOMATO SAUCE *(page 20)*

SEASONED BREADCRUMBS *(page 101)*

CREOLE RED GRAVY *(page 22)*
MEATBALLS *(page 143)*

STUFFED EGGPLANT *(page 47)*

BOURBON BALLS *(page 159)*

LEMON PECAN CORNMEAL CAKE *[page 167]*

CANNOLI *(page 160)*

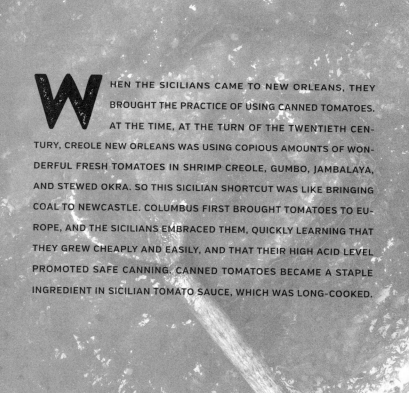

WHEN THE SICILIANS CAME TO NEW ORLEANS, THEY BROUGHT THE PRACTICE OF USING CANNED TOMATOES. AT THE TIME, AT THE TURN OF THE TWENTIETH CENTURY, CREOLE NEW ORLEANS WAS USING COPIOUS AMOUNTS OF WONDERFUL FRESH TOMATOES IN SHRIMP CREOLE, GUMBO, JAMBALAYA, AND STEWED OKRA. SO THIS SICILIAN SHORTCUT WAS LIKE BRINGING COAL TO NEWCASTLE. COLUMBUS FIRST BROUGHT TOMATOES TO EUROPE, AND THE SICILIANS EMBRACED THEM, QUICKLY LEARNING THAT THEY GREW CHEAPLY AND EASILY, AND THAT THEIR HIGH ACID LEVEL PROMOTED SAFE CANNING. CANNED TOMATOES BECAME A STAPLE INGREDIENT IN SICILIAN TOMATO SAUCE, WHICH WAS LONG-COOKED.

CREOLE RED GRAVY

The Creole staple Italianesque sauce also belongs in this chapter, because you cannot make an authentic meatball or Italian sausage po'boy without it. Creole New Orleanians just couldn't stand still and wait for Sicilian tomato sauce to slowly thicken, so they began thickening it with a roux. Roux changes the taste and the mouth feel of tomato sauce. This Creolized version is delicious, but it is clearly not Italian tomato sauce—it's Italian American. If you taste the two sauces side by side, the difference is marked.

This recipe uses the Creole adoption of canned tomato sauce. Tomatoes were common in early Creole cuisine, but canned tomatoes were not.

New Orleans–style Creole Red Gravy tastes best with meatballs, Italian sausage on a po'boy, or on meatloaf. If you want to go all the way with Louisiana flavors, make oyster spaghetti. About 10 minutes before you plan to serve your red gravy, throw in oysters, some of the oyster liquor, about 2 pounds of cooked crawfish tails, and the crawfish fat. Let this cook about 10 minutes and serve over spaghetti.

¼ cup bacon grease

¼ cup all-purpose flour

1 medium onion, chopped

1 clove garlic, minced

2 stalks celery, chopped

1 green bell pepper, chopped

3 scallions, chopped

3 (14-ounce) cans tomato sauce

¼ cup chopped parsley

1 tablespoon Creole Italian Seasoning Mix (recipe follows)

1 teaspoon dried thyme

1 teaspoon Louisiana hot sauce (or more to taste)

Salt and pepper to taste

For serving: cooked spaghetti and grated Italian cheese

1. Heat bacon grease over medium-low heat in a large pot with a heavy bottom. Slowly sauté flour, stirring constantly, until it is the color of café au lait, a medium-light brown. Add onion and garlic and cook 2 minutes. Add the celery, bell pepper, and scallions. When the vegetables are soft, add the tomato sauce. Stir and simmer, uncovered, 1 hour.

2. Add parsley, Creole Italian Seasoning Mix, thyme, and hot sauce. Salt and pepper to taste. Serve over spaghetti and top with grated cheese. This is a true Creole Italian meal.

CREOLE ITALIAN SEASONING MIX

Forget grocery-store Italian seasoning mixes. Make this and keep it ready for all of your Creole Italian needs.

Place all ingredients in a jar. Screw on the lid and shake thoroughly. Keep in a cool, dark place. Use liberally.

2 teaspoons crushed red pepper

2 teaspoons dried basil

2 teaspoons dried oregano

2 teaspoons dried parsley

1½ teaspoons ground anise or fennel seed

2 teaspoons dried whole thyme

QUASI RICOTTA (ALMOST RICOTTA)

MAKES ABOUT 4 CUPS

Nana used ricotta for so many things, and sometimes she ran out just when she needed it. Because she didn't drive, a trip to the store would mean a long walk or bus ride, so she would whip up this substitute. This is tasty cheese, and it should encourage us to think about how easy it is to make fresh cheeses of all kinds.

½ gallon pasteurized, unhomogenized whole milk, if you can find it. (Do not use ultra-pasteurized milk)

2 cups buttermilk

Cheesecloth

1. In a stainless steel pot, combine the milk and the buttermilk. Over low heat, stir the mixture slowly until it reaches 100°F. Stop stirring and let the mixture continue to heat. Curds should begin forming after 10 minutes. When the mixture reaches between 180–190°F, remove from the heat and cover. Let the pot rest to allow the curds to fully form, about 30 minutes. The whey should separate from the curds and gradually grow clearer.

2. Line a colander with cheesecloth and place it over another pot to catch the whey. Ladle in the curds and allow to drain about 15 or 20 minutes. At this point the cheese will be quite loose, but it will firm up in the refrigerator. Use a spoon to place the ricotta into a clean bowl and cover tightly with plastic wrap. Refrigerate. Use the whey to make bread, or use instead of water in vegetable soup.

WINE VINEGAR

MAKES AS MUCH AS YOU WANT

Another example of Nana's frugality was her collection of large jars that held wine vinegar in various stages of production. My grandmother never threw anything away if some value could be squeezed out of it. To her, it was a sin to waste food, and wine was food. So if anyone left wine in a glass or if there was just an inch left in the bottle, she would feed the vinegar jug. And she was such a sophisticated cook that she had both white wine and red wine vinegar jars going.

You can't make vinegar without adding a substance called mother of vinegar, which is a gelatinous mass of bacteria made from fermenting alcohol. Nana kept her mother of vinegar well fed, and it thrived. She'd share her supply with friends and family.

I find it gratifying to make my own vinegar. Homemade vinegar tastes good, and you have the satisfaction of knowing you're not wasting anything.

Before you begin your own batch, there are a few things to remember:

- Vinegar is alive, and it must be fed. If you forget about it, the bacteria that eats the alcohol sugars and converts them into vinegar will die of starvation. At least once a week feed a little wine to your mother of vinegar. If you must leave it for an extended trip and there's no one to feed it, put it in the refrigerator. The cold temperature will slow the process, and it will likely live until you return.

- You must make your vinegar in a large clean glass jar. About a half gallon is a good size. Do not use plastic. I like a wide-mouth jar for a couple of reasons: it doesn't require a funnel to add wine and it's wide enough for a ladle to fit in, which makes it easy to scoop out vinegar to fill bottles or use in cooking. To top your jar, you need cheesecloth and a rubber band.

Wine

Mother of vinegar

Glass jars, cheesecloth, and rubber bands

- You also need a starter, which often means buying a mother-of-vinegar culture. Many wine and beer-making shops sell a mother. It is also sold on the internet. If you buy it, smell it to make sure it smells like vinegar. If it doesn't smell like sharp vinegar, it has probably died. You can also ask a friend who makes wine vinegar to give you a bit of the mother. Or you can try making mother of vinegar from organic apple cider vinegar with live cultures. The bottle you buy should have a large raft of culture in the bottom. Remove the mother from the cider vinegar by hand or with a spoon and use it as described below. The bacteria in different bottles are not always the same. So, although this often works, don't use too much wine mother when trying to make an apple cider vinegar mother. Sometimes the bacteria are not compatible.

1. Sterilize a large glass jar. You'll need about a cup of wine for each ⅛ cup of starter. (You can use either red or white wine. If you use a red wine starter, it will turn white wine pink.) Place the starter into the jar and cover with the wine by at least 4 to 5 inches. If you use more wine, it is not a problem, it will just take a little longer to make the vinegar. Place 2 layers of cheesecloth over the mouth of the jar and hold it in place with the rubber band. Place the jar out of the sun in a dark corner of your counter or in a pantry. Leave the jar alone, but check it every few days; you can't let the mother get dry or sit out of the liquid. After 5 days the mixture should begin to smell less and less like wine and more like vinegar. If it starts smelling rotten, throw it away and start over.

2. After about 6 weeks, you will have good vinegar. To use the vinegar, push aside the raft made by the mother and scoop the vinegar out with a ladle, leaving the mother in the jar. It is not necessary to strain the vinegar, but if you want, you can use a coffee filter to remove tiny particles.

3. To keep vinegar constantly fermenting, add leftover wine to the jar. Ladle out fully fermented vinegar into a smaller sterilized jar or bottle so that you can keep making more in your vinegar jar. At some point the mother will grow too large. Then you should remove it, cut off a piece, and return that piece to the jar. Divide the remainder into pieces and give them to friends. Sharing will keep the art of frugality alive.

CHAPTER 2

FINDING A PLACE IN THEIR NEW LAND

Vegetables and Fruit

I do not envy God's paradise, because I am so satisfied to live in Sicily.
—Attributed to Federico II, Holy Roman Emperor and King of Sicily

Roughly between 1885 and 1915, life was extremely hard in Sicily, and had been for a while. It was during this difficult time that Sicilians sailed to New Orleans in droves. Most of those tens of thousands settled in the French Quarter and spilled out into the adjacent neighborhood of Tremé, which was historically the home of New Orleans's free people of color. Because of the high-density settlement pattern of Sicilians in the French Quarter, this neighborhood came to be called Little Palermo. Regardless of whether this description was intended unkindly, it did acknowledge the impact of immigrant Sicilians on the city.

These newly settled Sicilians came from a place with a strong food identity, and they found themselves in a new world that also had an established and strong culinary culture. Even though New Orleans food conventions were vastly different from those of the Sicilians, the disparate cooks and consumers had at least one thing in common: they respected food. That mutual reverence for good food provided a Sicilian entry point into the jobs and daily life of Creole New Orleans. Eventually the city's food culture also proved to be appreciative of the Sicilian influences, with Sicilians contributing greatly to the canon of Creole food.

Although many Sicilian immigrants worked in construction or on the wharves in shipping, a huge number of them and their immediate descendants were farmers, waiters, and restaurant workers. They peddled fruits and vegetables and groceries. They fished and they opened restaurants. They worked in just about any job associated with selling food, which required specific skills and offered a path into a society that often did not require English-language skills in order to maneuver.

Like many immigrants, they might have started with a food cart and saved their money to eventually invest in a store. Because there were so many immigrants, they could make a living by selling to each other, which made it easier to begin such entrepreneurship.

In Tremé, my Nana's family lived on Governor Nicholls Street. Although she was christened Elisabetta Lecce, her friends Americanized her name to Bessie. My Big Nana, as I called my great-grandmother, had nine children, some of whom were born in New Orleans. My great-grandfather, the French Market butcher, had fled deprivation in his place of origin, and working in the food industry gave him access to a precious commodity. I presume that feeding his large family was easier because of his profession.

THE FRENCH MARKET HUB

In the early twentieth century my great-grandfather working in the French Market likely saw opportunities to purchase imported fruits from other vendors. Citrus was exported from Sicily to the Port of New Orleans, and local Sicilians imported bananas and pineapple from Central America and the Caribbean. Perhaps he could even trade butchered meat that could no longer be sold for the vast assortment of fruits and vegetables.

The French Quarter began as trading grounds for Native Americans at a bend in the Mississippi River. Early French settlers bartered with Native Americans at this site, and gradually other commerce was transacted in the same place. It was the Spanish who covered the market to shade it from direct sun and who made attempts to make it more sanitary.

By the time of the Louisiana Purchase in 1803 the market was an important hub of the city, located near what was a thriving port adjacent to the French Quarter. Mark Twain described the French Market as a polyglot place full of color and activity. Twain spent years piloting a riverboat on the Mississippi and visited New Orleans time and again. From the middle of the nineteenth century, the market was frequented by Native American Houma, Chitimacha, and Natchez people. There were people from South and Central America, the West Indies, Africa, China, Italy, Germany, Spain, and France, as well as the local Creoles descended from the Spanish and French, Black Creoles, farmers and fishermen from Acadiana, and various Americans who traveled the river. As the twentieth century approached, Twain found the same vibrant array of people mixing in the French Market, as well as in neighborhoods, calling New Orleans an "energetic city."

In those early days, the City of New Orleans leased French Market stall space to those who could pay, and there were special halls for meat, open-air spaces for fruits and vegetables, and areas for grain and coffee and other dry goods. The international nature of the place was reflected in the goods for sale, which included filé, fish, vegetables, eggs, rice, sausages, and all manner of fruits.

The Sicilians who came in on the big wave at the beginning of the twentieth century sold vegetables and fruits from their own fields. They plied their trade as butchers and fishmongers, and sold imported goods from Italy, such as oil, cheese, and lemons, and the imported fruit from South America. As the enormous number of them settled in the French Quarter, they changed both the French Quarter and the only place to buy groceries most of them knew, the French Market.

Every day, my grandmother walked about two

miles to the French Market from Tremé. Her mother couldn't make the trip because she was home rolling pasta, cooking, washing, and cleaning for her houseful of children. Money was always tight, and the French Market offered the freshest and largest selections of food. It felt closest to what they had known in Palermo, and it could mean a quick visit to see her father at the butcher building.

PLANTING ROOTS

My mother told the story of her parents' courtship. The place where Nana met my grandfather, Francesco Baiamonte, is in dispute. My Papa said they met at church. My grandmother said they met at a party. (I think the more likely version is at a party.) While they courted, my Aunt Sarah, Nana's younger sister, acted as their constant companion and chaperone.

Francesco was born to Sicilian parents. Before he married my grandmother, as soon as he had earned enough money and was old enough, he formally changed his name to Frank. He wanted to be more American, and I remember him correcting family members who would slip into old childhood patterns and call him Francesco. Frank grew up in the Amite area, a heavily Sicilian agricultural region north of New Orleans. He left school early and moved to New Orleans when he was fourteen years old and began his working career as a bricklayer's apprentice.

Throughout his life he tried many odd jobs. At some point he found employment with a freight-forwarding company named Lusk, learning the trade and spending much of his day on the docks adjacent to Little Palermo, the French Quarter. The work was physically hard, but it was the best he could expect with only a fourth-grade education. He was always self-conscious about his lack of formal education,

Mr. and Mrs. Joseph Lecce
720 Barracks Street
request the honor of your presence
at the marriage of their daughter

Elisabeth

and

Mr. Frank Baiamonte

on the evening of Tuesday, the third of July
one thousand nine hundred and seventeen
at six o'clock
Saint Mary's Church
New Orleans

Nana and Papa's wedding invitation

and he tried to make up for it by reading, particularly works from the lists and lists of books he considered important. He had endless curiosity about the origins of everything, and it was from observing my Papa that I learned the difference between being intelligent and being educated. Those traits were not necessarily synonymous.

Papa and Nana married in July 1917 at St. Mary's Italian Church in the French Quarter. Following the Sicilian tradition of multigenerational living, the newlyweds moved in with the large family of Lecces. The Lecce home was a typical Tremé raised wooden cottage with a kitchen in the back. The house seemed

My mother and Nana in Tremé

siblings, and my grandfather grew close to everyone. The whole while, he worked and saved money to buy a house. After all, he and my grandmother were American, and home ownership was the American dream. A house would be a sign of their upward mobility and of their becoming more American. While they saved their money, my mother happily continued to live in this raucous household that spoke the Sicilian dialect. To this extended family there was little reason to speak Italian or any other language in their community; the language was Sicilian.

In time, three generations, two married children and spouses, and several unmarried children were living in that house. My Papa felt the need to move, not only out of the house but from the area. Even though my grandmother's old neighborhood provided the comfort of strong familial ties, more and more he wanted to be "American."

My Papa's mother had been pregnant with him when the family made their journey from Sicily to New Orleans, so he was born in Louisiana. But his family lived among the many Sicilian immigrants north of New Orleans in Tangipahoa Parish. His first language was Sicilian, and I do not doubt that his decision to move away from a Sicilian neighborhood was partially because of the overt prejudice against Sicilians.

With a surname like Baiamonte, there was no escaping my grandfather's heritage. That perceived stigma prompted Papa to leap into Americanization through home ownership, just as it had also encouraged him to change his name to Frank. So, the Baiamontes moved to the neighborhood known as Lakeview, which, at the time was relatively new and mostly middle-class. They bought a lot and had a house built. Frank eventually helped my mother's Aunt Vi and Aunt Vera and their families move to Lakeview too.

The Lakeview house was in the 6700 block of Canal

enormous to my child's eyes, but I think at most it had three bedrooms and that the parlors were converted into extra bedrooms. My other deep recollection was that my great-aunts constantly scoured everything clean to within an inch of its life. Cleaning, cleaning, cleaning was my memory of that house.

My mother was born in that spotless house in April 1918, and she grew up in it as a little sister to her aunts and uncles. She was practically the same age as her uncle Joseph, who was my grandmother's youngest brother and the baby of the Lecce family. For almost twenty years the growing Baiamonte family lived with the Lecces and my grandmother's eight

My mother, Josephine

Nana and Papa at the Canal
Boulevard house, 1958

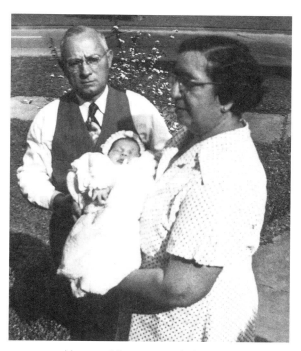

Nana and Papa at my christening

Boulevard. It was a typical two-bedroom, late 1930s home. Everyone shared one bathroom, but after living in the close quarters of the multigenerational Lecce house in Tremé, this new home probably felt spacious and peaceful. When visiting there I often explored my grandfather's reading materials. He owned the entire collection of the Harvard Classics, and he read and re-read them. He also had some of the Great Books series, but not the duplicates that were in the Harvard Classics.

My parents owned a house in the next block, in the 6800 block of Canal Boulevard, and this is where I grew up. This close proximity represented the compromise between living with my grandparents as my mother had, and living independently, which was more in line with the American dream of home ownership.

My mother was a little taller than her mother, although you can hardly call her tall at five feet two inches, and she had straight black hair and black eyes. As a young woman she was thin and loved clothes, and her main hobby was sewing and fashion. When I was a child, my still-slim mother would walk me to the corner and cross the side street, with me holding her hand. By the time we reached the other side, from down the sidewalk I could see my stout grandmother waving to me from the front of her house. At that point I would let go of my mother's hand and run to our destination. I loved visiting my grandmother.

OLD VEGETABLES IN A NEW WORLD

As I grew older, I would walk down the street by myself and help tend Nana's garden. I would also help myself to whatever she was cooking, which might be pasta, fish, meat, or chicken. And there were always lots of vegetables. My Papa tended the yard and grew a huge variety of vegetables in a garden that included a bay leaf tree, a huge fig tree, and three large Keifer pear trees that produced the hard pears my Nana used for canning. We ate most of the fresh vegetables he grew, while some were reserved to trade with other garden farmers who grew other things.

Papa's stunning array of vegetables put the grocery-store offerings of the day to shame, especially since the stores did not sell the majority of what my grandfather grew. (I didn't realize until I was a teenager that other people didn't eat broccoli rabe and cardoons.) The assortment of vegetables grown in the average Sicilian garden included arugula, radicchio, fennel, broccolini, chard, and lettuces. Just about everyone kept patches of parsley and basil. Not only was this bounty cooked in homes and shared with neighbors, but it was served at social gatherings. I remember a birthday party for a cousin, an age peer of my mother, and the fun of eating my way around the room. There was eggplant parmesan, artichokes in oil, fried artichokes, stuffed artichokes, cold cardoon salad, stewed fennel, raw fennel with various dips, fried and raw cauliflower, fried eggplant sticks, asparagus, broccoli rabe, radicchio, endive, many types of mushrooms, olive salad, pickled eggs, Japanese plums stuffed with gorgonzola, figs, and brandied kumquats. And that is only what I remember! There was also an abundance of meats and seafood at the party, but those things, although local, weren't homegrown.

Tomatoes were pretty common in New Orleans, but they were absolutely essential to my family's cooking. The tomato is a New World fruit, brought back to Europe as a part of the Columbian Exchange. Much of Europe had been slow to adopt the tomato as food, fearing it was toxic because it was related to the nightshade family. However, the always-starving Sicilians and the people of southern Italy embraced the "dangerous" fruit, and the tomato transformed their cuisine.

Another food from the Columbian Exchange is that

ubiquitous squash we associate with Italy, zucchini. Spanish conquistadores carried seeds of an early summer squash to Europe, and Italians planted lots of it. Through years of careful breeding and tending they developed what we now call zucchini.

Yet another squash, cucuzza, grows long, crooked, and almost freakishly fast. Cucuzza was grown in New Orleans by Sicilian immigrants and sold in the markets. It's sometimes hard to find in stores now. The risk for commercial farmers is that if it grows too large and too long, it develops a tough skin and huge, hard seeds. If you can get your hands on one, you'll find that cucuzza's mild flavor goes well cooked with other vegetables. If you come across it in a farmer's market or a friend's backyard, you should experiment.

In a less politically correct time, restaurants—including Italian restaurants owned by Italians—served a tasty romaine salad full of cheese, garlic, and olives which they called a "wop salad," using a slur that referred to Italians, especially southern Italians. Today restaurants serve an "Italian salad," but a few holdouts, such as Rocky and Carlos on St. Bernard Highway, still have "wop salad" on the menu.

Just as former Louisiana governor Edwin Edwards turned the slur "Cajun" into a term of pride, some people of Sicilian descent are now trying to throw the "wop" word back at the world. At Delmonico's there is a *guappo salad*. *Guappo* is said to be the origin of the word "wop," and it refers to a well-dressed, swaggering man more uppity than others think he has a right to be. In this context, the salad was swell, just like a person who was *guappo*. Another theory, now discredited, was that "wop" was an abbreviated form of "without papers," referring to the thousands of people who once came to these shores without immigration visas, but that designation would have applied to many others, not just Sicilians or other Italians.

There is probably enough lingering recollection of prejudice that retiring the "wop salad" is in order. But when Creole Italian restaurants do embrace it, it is a statement of pride and not prejudice. It is a measure of the deep roots of the Italians in our community, regardless of how American they have become.

A huge reason Sicilians grew their own vegetables in the early 1900s was because of the limited variety of produce in American markets. But as time went by, and grocery stores still didn't carry Sicilian produce, my aging grandparents and other immigrants gave up gardening, which meant that my mother and her peers stopped cooking that fantastic traditional assortment of vegetables. Fortunately, with our modern emphasis on "new" foods and a resurgence of cooking in general, these lovely, often bitter, vegetables have recently become popular. But for decades these foods were only in our diet when they were garden-grown.

A CALIFORNIA STATE OF MIND

It was in California where I learned about fresh produce that could be bought and not just gardened. My now husband, Rick, and I quit our studies at LSU and moved to San Francisco's Haight-Ashbury neighborhood to become hippies. Even though we were there on the waning side of the hippie movement, the influence of the fresh-food folks was evident everywhere. The abundance of fresh fruits and vegetables at the ordinary San Francisco grocery store was stunning.

I had always understood the goodness of fresh, but I had never seen it in the marketplace on a regular basis. My experience with fresh had only been in someone's garden, and this San Francisco vegetable phenomenon was eye-opening. There, I could buy figs, blackberries, and brussels sprouts without having to sweat or get my hands dirty. I was in heaven. I also

Rick and me

We humans always seem to seek balance, but to look at it from a different perspective always gives new ideas and tangents for exploration.

My only issue with those who worship freshness is that all too often, people think that eating fresh food is good enough. By starting with fresh ingredients, you have started with the best foundation, but you also have to consider taste. Let's discuss steamed crab, for example. In San Francisco I watched people flock to Fisherman's Wharf to eat steamed crab. My first time, I stood in line with anticipation. I'd grown up eating wonderful spicy boiled blue Gulf crabs in New Orleans, and I love crabmeat. So it was with an itch for pleasure that I brought that first bite of Dungeness crab to my waiting mouth. But no scratch was forthcoming. The crabmeat was bland—horribly so. And dipping it in butter just made it taste like butter. So the crab was fresh, but tasteless.

Too often in San Francisco I found that when the food was fresh, people were satisfied with flavorless. To them, flavor was not the point; the age of what they ate was what mattered. I, however, am always in search of flavor. Starting with fresh is a good first step, but without careful seasoning, freshness alone is not enough. Loving the taste of a fresh peach or a bowl of figs is definitely a pleasure. But steamed vegetables, no matter how fresh, are better with salt and pepper, oil or butter, and even a squirt of lemon juice or herbs. The art of cooking really is about intensifying flavor, especially when preparing something as bland as crab.

experimented with baking bread, eating sprouts of the "un-brussels" kind, as well as brown rice, whole wheat, tofu, and several grains I'd never heard of. I also experienced Asian flavors and ate Italian food from regions other than the tip of the boot.

We even toyed with vegetarianism, which was a joy, with such fantastic produce available. Rick was briefly macrobiotic, and I learned to create a macrobiotic meal for him that I could embellish. Fortunately, that foray into yin and yang food and its excessive discussion of the production of mucus did not last too long. But the lessons of balance, so overtly discussed, were valuable.

FRIED ARTICHOKES

1. Pull the tough outer leaves off the artichokes. Slice the bottom off the artichokes to about an inch below the heart and discard. Peel the stem and cut each artichoke into 8 to 10 pieces, cutting through from stem end to thorny tip. With a paring knife, cut away the choke. (Sometimes a grape-fruit knife helps.) Squeeze the lemon into a bowl of water and then add the lemon peels. Place the cut pieces of artichoke into the acidulated water to keep them from browning.

2. Add 3 inches of oil into a heavy pot and heat over medium-high heat. The oil is hot enough if it sizzles when you drop in a few breadcrumbs. If it burns and smokes, the oil is too hot. In that case, reduce the heat and wait a few minutes, then test again. You need to have the oil ready when the artichokes are ready to fry.

3. While the oil is heating, place the flour in a paper bag. Break the eggs into a bowl, add the water, and whip them together. Place the breadcrumbs in another bag. With this assembly line in place, dry the artichoke pieces well. Place a piece of artichoke in the paper bag with the flour and shake it gently to completely coat. Shake off the excess flour and dip the floured piece of artichoke in the egg wash to coat. Shake the piece of artichoke in the bag with the seasoned breadcrumbs.

4. When all the pieces of artichoke are ready, place a few into the oil and fry them until they are browned all over, about 6 minutes. Do not crowd them while they're frying. Drain the cooked artichokes on paper towels. Serve with *agliata* for dipping.

2 fresh artichokes

1 lemon

Peanut oil or other vegetable oil for frying

1 cup all-purpose flour

2 large eggs

2 tablespoons water

2 cups Seasoned Breadcrumbs (recipe page 101 or purchased)

For serving: Agliata (recipe page 102)

SHAVED ARTICHOKE SALAD

MAKES 6 TO 8 SERVINGS

1. Squeeze the lemon into the water and add the lemon rind. Pull the tough outer leaves off each artichoke and discard. Trim a third off the bottom stem of each artichoke. Working with one artichoke at a time, cut artichokes in half lengthwise. Slice them thinly on a mandoline, placing the flat side against the mandoline blade. Add the slices to the acidulated water to keep from discoloring.

2. In a serving bowl, combine the minced garlic and the olive oil and season with salt and pepper. Drain the artichokes. If you have a salad spinner, use it to get the artichokes as dry as possible. Add the dry artichoke slices and olives into the bowl with the dressing. Toss gently and cover with cling wrap.

3. Refrigerate the artichoke salad an hour before serving. Just before serving toss in the Parmesan cheese and top with the optional orange segments and chopped black olives.

½ a lemon

Bowl of water

35 to 40 small artichokes, usually called baby artichokes

5 cloves garlic, minced

½ cup good extra-virgin olive oil

Salt and pepper to taste

¼ cup chopped black olives

2–3 ounces Parmesan cheese, shaved

For serving: optional orange supremes* from 1 orange and ½ cup roughly chopped black olives cured in olive oil

*Supremes are orange segments that include only the orange flesh and none of the white pith.

STUFFED ARTICHOKES

MAKES 4 SERVINGS

In New Orleans, stuffed artichokes are found in most Creole Italian restaurants and are available as ready-to-eat takeout in many grocery stores. They also have a prominent place on St. Joseph altars. As you can tell by this recipe, the dish calls for simple ingredients, but putting them together takes a lot of work. Like so much Sicilian food, the flavor lies in the care and detail and not in expensive ingredients.

Bread was important to early New Orleans Sicilians, and even stale bread was valued. Stuffing vegetables with bread and seasonings still is a way to use up breadcrumbs and expand vegetables to be an entire meal.

My Aunt Jerry was a feisty handful. Her husband, Buster, was not Italian; he was Yugoslavian. When he made her angry, she'd remind him of this defect. But in spite of his ethnic shortcomings, he was extremely handy. He could fix or build any bicycle, and he was the inventor of my grandmother's fabulous bread-grating box. I loved that bread box, and I loved that Uncle Buster was always tinkering with something. I can remember watching him work on things, and my Aunt Jerry making breadcrumbs.

When I grew up, I became a lawyer. Whenever my Aunt Jerry had a question about her social security letter or a letter from the insurance company or some such thing, she would call me to her house. I was the family consigliere. In payment for my services I would receive something that contained breadcrumbs. My favorite was stuffed artichokes with lots of olive oil and cheese.

There was a ritual to these sessions. First came the telephone call. "I know that you haven't made stuffed artichokes for your husband and he likes them," she would say. "You are right, Aunt Jerry," I'd reply. "I haven't made stuffed artichokes. Are you offering?" "You know I do not usually have time to make stuffed artichokes for you. But I will make some for you because my stuffed artichokes are better than the ones my sister, your grandmother, made, and I want you to keep your husband. Come over at 5:00."

I would drive to Aunt Jerry's house, usually bringing my notarial seal, just in case. I would always go prepared to read documents and to eat.

The symmetry of these outings was reassuring. After rounds of kisses, catching up from the last visit, and discussions of other sundry family gossip, it was time to sit at her table. I had to eat whatever she had, which could be eggplant parmesan, some veal dish, shrimp, or squid. I was not allowed to refuse, and I had to clean my plate to establish that I really liked it. No burping was required. But a bit of dribbling would show that I had abandoned restraint, overcome by the goodness of the food.

To pay for my supper I then had to read and interpret her document or give some sort of legal advice. Usually the issue was easily resolved and explained in short order, and I would be on my way with four artichokes stuffed with breadcrumbs, cheese and spices, olive oil and garlic. I would ooh and ahh over my gift, kiss everyone who was there, and then leave. This happened about every three months, until my Aunt Jerry grew too ill to cook. No one has taken her place.

Now my family just asks me for legal advice without thinking it necessary to give me food. (It isn't necessary to give me food.) Although I felt like I was living in a *Godfather* movie when I sat at Aunt Jerry's house, I knew this was truly the old way, the honorable way for her to ask me for help without being beholden. She had the self-respect to want to repay for advice. She knew she was giving me something I valued but would not take the time to do myself. By the time I'd leave, the slate was always as clean as my plate.

1. Heat ½ cup olive oil in a heavy Dutch oven. (Do not use cast iron unless it is enameled.) Add the anchovy and stir it and break it up until it dissolves in the oil. Add the onion and sauté until the onions are soft, about 5 minutes. Add the garlic and sauté 30 seconds. Stir in the wine and the lemon juice. Place the breadcrumbs in a large bowl. Add the olive oil mixture and stir until it is well distributed.

2. To the Dutch oven, add 1 inch of water with remaining ¼ cup olive oil, a lemon half, and the bay leaves. Set aside.

3. Use a long, serrated knife to cut the pointy end off each artichoke. Cut the stems even with the base of the artichokes so they will sit well and upright in the pot and on the plate. Use a pair of scissors or a knife to remove any remaining thorns and remove any damaged leaves. Open the leaves like a flower and remove the choke. Rub the cut parts of the artichoke with the remaining lemon half and sprinkle the chokes with the salt.

4. Starting from the outside, fill the cavity of each leaf with the moistened breadcrumbs. As you reach the artichoke's center the leaves will be too small or too tight to stuff. At this point stuff the cavity in the center where the choke had been. Repeat this process with each artichoke, using all of the breadcrumbs. It should take a quarter of the mixture for each artichoke.

5. Preheat oven to 325°F. Place the artichokes into the Dutch oven. Cover and bring to a simmer. Place the hot pot into oven and bake until the leaves can easily be pulled off the artichokes, between 1¼ to 1½ hours. Place each artichoke on a plate. Garnish each with a slice of lemon on the top, and sprinkle with chopped parsley and lemon zest.

¾ cup olive oil, divided

1 anchovy

1 medium onion, finely chopped

6 cloves garlic, minced

½ cup dry white wine

2 tablespoons lemon juice

6 cups Seasoned Breadcrumbs (recipe page 101 or purchased)

2 lemon halves

2 bay leaves

A few cups water

4 large artichokes

1 teaspoon salt

For serving: 4 lemon slices, chopped fresh parsley, and lemon zest

ASPARAGUS IN OIL

MAKES 8 SERVINGS (3 OR 4 JARS)

These are great for parties and make a wonderful garnish in a Bloody Mary. I use the trimmed stems in salads that I dress with oil from the jar.

1. Trim the asparagus so that the entire stem fits in 3 or 4 sterilized pint or quart jars. If the bottoms of the stems are tender, they can be cut into salad sized pieces and preserved in jars also.

2. Use a pot wide enough for the entire length of the asparagus. Add the water, vinegar, salt, 1 teaspoon peppercorns, and a bay leaf and bring to a boil. Reduce heat to a simmer and carefully add the asparagus spears. Simmer until barely tender, 2 or 3 minutes.

3. Remove the spears to a clean dish cloth. If you're keeping the cut stems, add them to the simmering water and cook about 3 minutes. Remove to a clean dish cloth.

4. To each of the jars add 5 to 10 peppercorns and 1 small bay leaf. Divide the blanched asparagus among the jars, with the delicate flower end pointing up. Add olive oil to completely cover and screw on the jar lids. The cut stems can also be placed into a jar and covered with olive oil. Place the jars into the refrigerator. Cure at least 2 weeks. The oil will congeal.

5. Just before serving, remove enough spears for each serving plate and allow them to return to room temperature. The oil will liquefy.

2 pounds raw green asparagus, not too skinny

1 cup water

1 cup white wine vinegar or champagne vinegar

2 teaspoons sea salt

1 teaspoon peppercorns, plus more for each jar

1 bay leaf for the pot, plus 1 more for each jar

Extra-virgin olive oil

STUFFED BELL PEPPERS

MAKES 4 SERVINGS

These peppers are a far cry from the traditional southern stuffed bell pepper, especially since there is no rice. My father, whose go-to starch was rice, actually grew to prefer these breadcrumb-stuffed bell peppers over the rice-stuffed ones of his childhood. I always wondered if his change in taste came about because his mother wasn't a good cook or because he just loved my mother. Regardless, he was enthusiastic about them.

1. Preheat oven to 325°F. Slice the bell peppers in half, cutting through the stem. With a small knife, trim away the ribs and remove the seeds. Set the peppers aside.

2. Add the olive oil to a sauté pan set over medium heat. Add the onions and caramelize them slightly, about 5 minutes. Add the celery to the onions and cook another 5 minutes. Add the sausage, breaking it up as you cook. When the sausage is done, add the shrimp and crabmeat and stir well.

3. Place the mixture, including the oil, into a large bowl to cool. Add the breadcrumbs and mix everything together well. If the mixture is dry and does not stick together, add a bit of water or white wine until moist. Divide the stuffing evenly among the 4 pepper halves, spooning it compactly. Mound the mixture if necessary. Sprinkle the tops with the grated cheese. Place the stuffed peppers into a small dish and bake until tops are deep brown, about 45 minutes. Serve with tomato sauce or Creole red gravy.

2 bell peppers of any color

3 tablespoons olive oil

½ cup chopped onion

¼ cup chopped celery

½ cup sweet Italian sausage, removed from its casing

½ cup chopped cooked shrimp

½ cup picked crabmeat

2 cups Seasoned Breadcrumbs (recipe page 101 or purchased)

¼ cup grated Parmesan cheese

For serving: Nana's Basic Tomato Sauce (recipe page 20) or Creole Red Gravy (recipe page 22)

SWEET PIMENTOS IN OIL

MAKES ABOUT 3 PINTS

1. Broil the peppers, turning every few minutes so that all the sides of the peppers have blistered skin and are turning black. Alternatively, the peppers can be blackened on a grill or even directly over a gas burner (although this can be messy, it was Nana's preferred method). Place the hot blackened peppers into a heavy paper bag and fold closed. Allow them to steam inside the bag at least 10 minutes.

2. When the peppers are cool enough to handle, place them in a colander. Pull off the stems and pull out the seeds. Drain away the liquid. Pull the blackened and blistered skin from the peppers and discard it. Cut the peeled peppers into strips.

3. Place the water, vinegar, and salt into a pot and heat the mixture until it boils. Put the pepper strips into a glass bowl or large jar and pour the vinegar mixture over it. Cover the bowl with a plate or plastic wrap and leave in the refrigerator 2 hours.

4. Drain the peppers and distribute them among 3 pint jars. Depending on the size of the peppers, you might need a fourth jar. Fill the jars with olive oil. Distribute the capers among the jars. Replace lids and refrigerate.

About 12 sweet bell peppers, all one color or assorted

1 cup water

1 cup white wine vinegar or champagne vinegar

2 teaspoons sea salt

Extra-virgin olive oil

2 tablespoons small capers in salt

FRIED CAULIFLOWER

1. In a large pot bring the water to a boil. Divide the raw cauliflower into small florets and parboil them, 2 minutes. Remove cauliflower with a spider or a slotted spoon and place them directly in the ice bath to stop the cooking. When they have all been removed, drain the florets and dry them well.

2. After cauliflower is dry, add at least 3 inches oil to a heavy pot and heat over medium-high heat. The oil is hot enough when a puff of flour sizzles when you throw it into the oil.

3. Place flour in a paper bag. Break the eggs into a bowl with the water and whip them together. Place the breadcrumbs in another bag. With this assembly line in place, place a cauliflower floret in the paper bag with the flour and shake it gently to completely coat. Shake off the excess flour and dip the floret in the egg wash. Place the floret in the paper bag with the seasoned breadcrumbs and shake to coat.

4. When all the florets are coated, place a few into the oil and fry them until they are browned all over, about 5 to 6 minutes, depending on size. Do not crowd while they're frying. Drain cooked cauliflower on paper towels. Serve with *agliata* for dipping.

Water for boiling

1 head cauliflower

Ice bath in a large bowl

Peanut oil or other vegetable oil for frying

1 cup all-purpose flour

2 large eggs

2 tablespoons water

2 cups Seasoned Breadcrumbs (recipe page 101 or purchased)

For serving: Agliata (recipe page 102)

FRIED EGGPLANT STICKS

MAKES 4 SERVINGS

Fried eggplant sticks are a favorite snack found on menus of many Creole restaurants. Some restaurants do not mix cheese with the bread-crumbs, but otherwise they are almost the same everywhere. Instead of *agliata*, Creole restaurants typically serve them with béarnaise sauce. They are also famously served dusted with powdered sugar.

I secretly believe that old-line restaurants Creolized this Italian fa-vorite. My family uses breadcrumbs with cheese, but if you prefer you can use breadcrumbs without cheese. And if the eggplant was served as a vegetable for the meal, my family didn't use powdered sugar. But if fried eggplant sticks were appetizers at a party, there would be plenty of powdered sugar sprinkled over them.

Many traditional recipes call for salting and draining the eggplant to remove excess water. Some say this extra step reduces bitterness. That may have been true decades ago, but modern eggplants have been bred to avoid bitterness, so I think this step can be omitted. Not soaking also produces fluffier and more tender eggplant sticks. When frying, you want to be sure the temperature of the oil is really hot enough; eggplant soaks up oil if the temperature is too low.

1 large firm eggplant

Peanut oil or other vegetable oil for frying

1 cup all-purpose flour

2 large eggs

2 tablespoons water

2 cups Seasoned Breadcrumbs (recipe page 101 or purchased)

For serving: Agliata (recipe page 102)

1. Use a vegetable peeler to peel the eggplant. Slice the eggplant into thick French fry–like sticks.

2. Add at least 3 inches oil to a heavy pot and heat over medium-high heat. The oil is hot enough when you throw in a puff of flour and the oil sizzles.

3. Meanwhile, place the flour in a paper bag. Break the eggs into a bowl, add the water, and whip them together. Next to the eggs, place the breadcrumbs in another bag. With this assembly line in place, place a few eggplant sticks in the paper bag with the flour and shake it gently to completely coat. Shake off the excess flour and dip the eggplant sticks in the egg wash. Then shake the eggplant sticks with the seasoned breadcrumbs.

4. When all the eggplant sticks are fully coated, place a few into the hot oil and fry until they are browned all over. Do not crowd them while they're cooking, and turn only once. Drain cooked eggplant sticks on paper towels. Serve immediately with *agliata*.*

*The bread and garlic sauce known as *agliata* is not flavored with tarragon, as is the béarnaise sauce that traditionally accompanies fried eggplant sticks in New Orleans restaurants. But adding ground anise or fennel seeds to *agliata* would make it a close cousin to béarnaise.

PARMIGIANA DI MELANZANE (EGGPLANT PARMESAN)

MAKES 4 TO 6 SERVINGS

This dish, so dear to Sicilians, was the precursor to veal parmesan. Eggplant grows well in Sicily, and is the basis of caponata and eggplant parmesan. When Sicilians came to America, they thought the meat here was abundant and cheap, in contrast to the prohibitively expensive meat available in Sicily. In America, those lucky enough to afford meat for feast day celebrations found they could substitute meaty eggplant slices with actual meat, so eggplant parmesan gave birth to veal parmesan. When that happened, eggplant parmesan became demoted to a side dish, but it is a glorious one and can easily be a satisfying meatless meal.

1. Preheat your oven to 325°F. Slice the unpeeled eggplants into rounds about ¼ inch thick. Lay the slices in several colanders and sprinkle them liberally with salt. Wait 30 minutes. Some of the liquid in the eggplants should have drained away. Rinse the slices to remove the excess salt. Pat them dry and dredge in the flour.

2. Heat about 1 inch of vegetable oil in a frying pan or wok until it's hot and fry batches of the floured eggplant slices until browned, turning at least once, about 5 minutes. (Add more oil as necessary.) Drain on paper towel. After all the eggplant is fried, prepare the sauce.

3. Make a sauce by adding the olive oil to a pot and heat until hot. Sauté the garlic in the oil until it is soft, about 2 minutes. Stir in the tomato puree and Creole Italian Seasoning Mix and cook 10 minutes over medium heat, stirring occasionally. If it becomes too thick, add water or wine. Remove from heat.

4. Place 3 spoons of tomato sauce into a gratin pan and spread to cover the bottom. Add 1 layer of fried eggplant. Add more tomato sauce, some of the mozzarella and some of the Parmigiano. Continue making layers until all of the ingredients are used up, ending with the mozzarella, then the Parmigiano.

5. Bake until bubbly and the cheese is melted, at least 30 minutes. Let sit 10 minutes before serving.

2 medium firm eggplants

Salt

Seasoned flour for dredging

Vegetable oil for frying (do not use expensive olive oil, just a neutral oil)

2 tablespoons olive oil

3 cloves garlic, minced

2 cups tomato puree

2 tablespoons Creole Italian Seasoning Mix (recipe page 23)

Up to 1 cup water or leftover wine

¾ cup shredded whole-milk mozzarella

1 cup grated Parmigiano cheese

STUFFED EGGPLANT

MAKES 2 SERVINGS

1. Heat your oven to 325°F. Slice the unpeeled eggplant in half lengthwise. With a melon baller, scoop out the meat of the eggplant, leaving a "boat" with about ½ inch on the sides. Brush the insides and outsides of the boats with olive oil.

2. Pour a few tablespoons olive oil in a hot skillet and sauté the eggplant pulp until soft. Add the onion and celery and continue to cook until softened. Add the Italian sausage, shrimp, and crabmeat. Remove from heat and stir in the breadcrumbs. Mix thoroughly, moistening with extra olive oil as needed.

3. Divide the stuffing between the two eggplant boats. Place 2 slices of tomato on top of each and sprinkle on the grated Parmesan cheese. Place the 2 stuffed eggplant halves into a casserole dish and cover with aluminum foil. Bake 1 hour. Remove the foil and cook an additional 15 minutes. Serve warm.

1 medium or large firm eggplant

Olive oil

½ cup chopped onion

¼ cup chopped celery

½ cup sweet Italian sausage, removed from casing

½ cup chopped cooked shrimp

½ cup picked crabmeat

2 cups Seasoned Breadcrumbs (recipe page 101 or purchased)

4 slices fresh tomato

¼ cup grated Parmesan cheese

FRITEDDA (SAUTÉED SPRING VEGETABLES)

MAKES 4 TO 6 SERVINGS

Fritedda is one of my favorite dishes. Clifford A. Wright, a Sicilian food historian, has suggested a relationship between *fritedda* and some Middle Eastern–inspired appetizers. Maybe this luscious combination of vegetables hails from the time of the Arab conquest of Sicily. After all, it was the Arabs who brought the artichoke to Sicily, as well as the scallion. Regardless, the island has been conquered so many times that its food and entire culture tell a complex and deep story.

I cannot remember not loving *fritedda*. It's rather a chore to make, especially when starting with large globe artichokes. And then there is the shelling of the fava beans and the peas. But as a child I requested this dish for every special occasion—my birthday, a family gathering, a special anything. I always considered this dish a gift from my mother. I cannot eat it without thinking of her.

When cherry tomatoes were available, my mother would halve 10 to 15 of them and add them to the pan when she added the artichokes. I loved it either way. The addition of tomatoes was not traditional, but it showed my mother's creeping Creolization. After all, she had been born and raised in New Orleans.

4 fresh globe artichokes or 12 baby artichokes

1 lemon

Bowl of water

½ cup olive oil

4 shallots, finely minced

5 scallions, thinly sliced

5 cloves garlic, finely minced

1 pound shelled baby fava beans

1 pound shelled peas

¼ cup sherry vinegar

2 tablespoons chopped capers

Salt and pepper to taste

½ cup chopped fresh mint

¼ cup toasted pine nuts

For serving: ½ cup raisins or currants and freshly grated nutmeg (both optional)

1. If using globe artichokes, snip off the sharp points of the leaves, remove any tough outer leaves, and remove the interior thistle. Cut the trimmed globe artichokes into eighths, cutting through from stem end to thorny tip. If using baby artichokes, remove the ends of the leaves if they are tough and thorny, and cut the trimmed artichokes into quarters. Squeeze the lemon into a large bowl of water and add the skins. Place the artichokes into the acidulated water.

2. Place the olive oil in a large frying pan and heat on medium heat. Add the shallots, scallions, and garlic and cook until translucent, about 5 minutes. Drain the artichokes and add them to the pan. Sautee the artichokes, heating them through but keeping them crisp, about 4 or 5 minutes. Add the fava beans and peas, then stir in the sherry vinegar and capers. Stir and cook 2 or 3 minutes.

3. Adjust for salt and pepper and transfer to a platter. Sprinkle with mint and pine nuts. The dish can also be garnished with raisins and dusted with nutmeg. Serve hot or at room temperature.

GIARDINIERA (PICKLED VEGETABLES) WITH OKRA

MAKES ABOUT 2 QUARTS

Okra came to New Orleans with the African slave trade. My mother did not grow up eating much of it, and she definitely was not a fan. My father, however, who was a child of the American South, loved okra in its many forms. I loved it too.

My mother made every attempt to like okra. She fried it and stewed it and used it in gumbo, but she only tolerated it. She finally found a way to enjoy it: she adapted her *giardiniera* recipe to include okra. Her recipe is the perfect marriage of Italian pickled vegetables and pickled okra. My father liked the way she made these pickles but was always urging her to add more okra.

1. Place the vegetables in a nonreactive bowl and toss thoroughly with salt. Add water to cover, cover the bowl, and allow the vegetables to brine 12 hours in refrigerator. Drain and rinse, and drain again.

2. In a sterilized quart jar, add all the vinaigrette ingredients. Cover the jar and shake. When thoroughly mixed, divide the vinaigrette into 2, using a second jar. Divide the drained vegetables between the 2 jars, making sure to not overload a particular vegetable in one jar. Make sure one garlic clove is in each jar, as well as 1 bay leaf. The vinaigrette should cover the vegetables in each jar. If you need more vinaigrette, make more.

3. Cover and refrigerate. After a week, the *giardiniera* is ready to eat. This must be kept refrigerated.

10 (3-inch or smaller) very fresh okra

2 sweet red bell peppers, cleaned and cut into 1-inch sticks

4 whole, small hot peppers

3 stalks celery, cut into 1-inch sticks

3 large carrots, cut into 1-inch sticks

1 medium cauliflower, cut into small florets

½ cup salt

Water

VINAIGRETTE

2 cups white vinegar

2 cloves garlic, slivered

2 bay leaves

3 teaspoons dried oregano or Italian seasoning

1 teaspoon red pepper flakes

1 teaspoon crushed black peppercorns

½ teaspoon celery seeds or fennel seeds

½ teaspoon whole coriander seeds

INSALATA DI ARANCE (ORANGE SALAD)

MAKES 6 SERVINGS

Peel the oranges and remove as much pith as possible. Cut the oranges into supremes (sections) (see note on page 36). Place the orange supremes into a serving bowl and add the fennel slices, onion slices, and olives. Add the olive oil, lemon juice, and parsley. Toss the salad then add the croutons, salt, and pepper. Toss again and top with the reserved fennel fronds and the fennel seed. Bring to the table for serving.

4 navel oranges

2 bulbs fennel, sliced thinly (reserve fronds)

1 red onion, sliced thinly

½ cup black pitted olives

6 tablespoons olive oil

Juice of ½ lemon

2 tablespoons fresh, chopped Italian parsley

1 cup cornbread croutons

Salt and pepper to taste

2 teaspoons fennel seed

COOKING-PEAR SALAD

MAKES 8 SERVINGS

This is a good way to use old-fashioned Kieffer cooking pears without having to cook them. Surprisingly, when diced these pears are crispy and sweet and easy to chew. In this recipe they complement the bitterness of the radicchio, and the colors make a pretty salad. Lots of backyards in New Orleans have a fast-growing Kieffer pear tree or two, and they can be prolific. The large, yellow, oval-shaped fruit has a crisp, coarse flesh that makes a nice pear butter I like to flavor with cardamom, lemon peel, and ginger. They are also good in a pie. But sometimes you want something light and fresh, and this dish hits the spot.

4 large cooking pears, peeled and diced

1 head radicchio, torn

2 stalks celery, diced

½ cup whole, pitted black olives

½ cup Olive Oil and Lemon Spread (recipe page 16), at room temperature

Place all the ingredients in a large salad bowl and toss together well. If the spread is too thick to mix in easily, add the juice of half of a lemon.

STUFFED TOMATOES

MAKES 4 SERVINGS

St. Bernard and Plaquemines Parishes are downriver of New Orleans, and farmers in this region produce wonderful Creole tomatoes. While the variety of tomato can vary, the tomatoes grown in the rich alluvial soil lining the Mississippi River and under the open sky produce what we know as a Creole tomato. The LSU Agricultural School tried to produce a tomato that tasted like a Creole tomato, no matter where it was grown. But like the Vidalia onion and other vegetables that reflect *terroir,* the place they are grown, it is the soil, the environment, the rainfall, etc., that make a Creole tomato taste uniquely good.

A Creole tomato is a far cry from the meaty Roma tomato familiar to the Sicilians before they came here. The firm Roma is best for cooking down into thick pasta sauce, while the juicy Creole is best for slicing, and is extremely good stuffed.

2 large Creole tomatoes

Olive oil

Salt and pepper to taste

2 cups Seasoned Breadcrumbs (recipe page 101 or purchased)

½ cup grated Parmesan cheese

1. Preheat your oven to 350°F. Cut each tomato into 2 through the stem end. Use a spoon to scoop the pulp and seeds out of the halves. Chop the tomato pulp, seeds and all, and place it and any juice that may have leaked onto the cutting board into a bowl.

2. Brush the 4 tomato halves inside and out with olive oil and sprinkle the halves with salt and pepper. Mix the breadcrumbs with the chopped tomato and juice. Divide the stuffing among the tomato halves. Top each with Parmesan cheese. Bake until crispy brown on top, at least 45 minutes. Serve warm.

TURNIP GREENS

MAKES 4 TO 6 SERVINGS

The myriad of food parallels between Sicily and New Orleans never ceases to amaze me. For example, it is a common practice for Sicilians to have cooked bitter greens ready in the refrigerator. They typically use these greens tossed with pasta and cheese, as a garnish for a quick meal of warmed-over soup, or as a side dish for leftover roasted chicken. Many a southerner also has cooked greens in the refrigerator for any of these eventualities.

Even though Sicilians often turned to broccoli rabe or radicchio, my father's favorite green was turnip greens. This is the recipe my mother made for him.

My dad loved to eat a light supper or even a breakfast of warmed-up greens with potlikker, which he would sop up with cornbread. Although turnip greens were his favorite, he loved any type of greens. They can all be prepared the same way. If you have experienced really tough greens that take forever to cook and have the texture of leather, it is because the leaves were big and stayed on the plant a long time. To remedy this problem, chiffonade the leaves as finely as you can before you cook them. Cutting them into small pieces helps reduce the toughness and cuts the cooking time.

If you keep a bottle of tiny hot peppers in vinegar by the stove or on the table, you can use that vinegar and omit the hot sauce. I like to use plain vinegar, not pepper vinegar, so that I can control the burn.

1 pound cleaned turnip greens (You can substitute any type of greens or a mixture, even kale.)

¼ cup bacon fat

1 medium onion, chopped

10 cloves garlic, sliced

¼ pound ham, chopped

¼ cup white vinegar

1 tablespoon hot sauce

Salt and pepper to taste

1. Remove any large stems from the greens and discard. Chop the cleaned greens. Heat the bacon fat in a large skillet. When it's hot, add the onion and sauté until they are soft, about 5 minutes. Add the garlic and ham and cook 2 minutes. Add the turnip greens. Toss to help reduce the volume.

2. Cover and allow to steam 3 minutes. Uncover and toss again. Wait 3 minutes. Uncover and toss again. By this time the volume of the greens should be greatly reduced. Add the vinegar and hot sauce. Toss again and cook, uncovered and stirring occasionally, until the greens reach your desired doneness. Adjust for salt and pepper. Remember that the bacon fat and the ham are salty. The hot sauce might make black pepper superfluous.

CHAPTER 3

PREJUDICE AND PASTA

Pasta and Starches

What happened to those eleven Italians, it was wrong, and the city owes them and their descendants a formal apology. At this late date, we cannot give justice. But we can be intentional and deliberate about what we do going forward. This attack was an act of anti-immigrant violence. New Orleans is a welcoming city. . . . But there remain serious and dark chapters to our shared story that remain untold and unaccounted for.
—New Orleans Mayor LaToya Cantrell, April 12, 2019

Although most early twentieth-century Sicilians had education levels on par with their American peers, Sicilians were paid the lowest wages. The wage disparity may have been because of their language issues, or maybe they represented the classic threat of the immigrant: they entered the city in such large numbers that their presence was glaringly apparent. Or maybe it's because their cultural practices were different, and they would assemble and maintain their traditions and language without immediately assimilating. To counter the unfair-wage problem, Sicilian immigrants invested together through benevolent societies that created businesses that hired more Sicilians. This prac-tice helped to steady wages, but it did little to ease their outsider status.

By my generation, the French Quarter was no lon-ger Little Palermo, which had been essentially a Sicilian ghetto. Gone were the macaroni factories that had churned out fettuccini, spaghetti, and fusilli that fed the longing of the masses of transplanted Sicilians. Gone, too, from the French Quarter were the thou-sands of Sicilians who had been living in this, the old-est part of the city. A historic preservation movement had long taken hold of the impoverished area, and property values had improved. But even though things were physically looking better by the time I was born, a strong, dark memory of prejudice against Sicilians still lingered inside my mother.

The famous lynching of Sicilians living in New Orleans had happened in 1891. There is some controversy about the details, but after the killing of Police Chief David Hennessy, eleven of the city's men of Sicilian heritage were executed by a mob, presumably in retaliation for the chief's murder. Some of those lynched were acquitted at trial. My mother was born in 1918, and those twenty-seven intervening years had been too short to calm my family's fears. And prejudice would indeed rear its frightening head when she attended St. Mary's Italian Church in the French Quarter and when she shopped in the French Market and the French Quarter with their many Sicilian businesses.

But my mother grew up in the comfortable Sicilian community that had expanded into Tremé, and this neighborhood was thankfully different. In her friendly section of the city she attended St. Ann School, and while there she not only associated with other Sicilians but also developed a special bond that united her with the African Americans living in area. The older Italian women in Tremé had schooled me on the trust they had in their African American neighbors. Even in the 1950s, before my parents put me into public school, I attended two years of Catholic grammar school in Tremé. After school I would walk to the home of my great-aunt Sarah, who was living in what had been my Big Nana's house, and I would stay there until my parents picked me up after work. I played with the children in the neighborhood, no matter the color or nationality, and we visited each other's houses. Aunt Sarah had a huge freezer filled with huckabucks, Kool-Aid frozen in a paper Dixie cup, and she'd share them with all the kids. Neither my aunt nor my Nana could pronounce the word "huckabuck." It came out "huck-

abucka." We children called them that too. (See page 169 for the recipe.)

My mother recalled instances of prejudice, which I certainly did not experience daily. But I did encounter it occasionally, and when it happened I was always surprised.

One of the most memorable slights my mother encountered was when she went to LSU in Baton Rouge as a freshman and was not allowed to join a sorority. Because her last name was Baiamonte, she was marked as Sicilian, and was therefore unwelcome in the sororities. My mother had always had to fight not to be held back by her extended family because she was a girl. She was gifted in math and was often the only girl in her math classes, so after high school she went to college. After great pressure from her aunts, who thought she was selfish for "wasting" her parents' money educating a girl, she dropped out of LSU and went to "beauty school" and became a hairdresser.

When my time came for college, my mother wanted me to join a sorority, I suppose in some respects to live vicariously through my experience. Of course, times were vastly different when I attended LSU in the last years of the 1960s. I, like so many others, was caught up in the flower child movement and protests against the Vietnamese War. The last thing I wanted to do was to join a sorority. But I did. For my mother.

I pledged a sorority my freshman year, but I quickly learned I wasn't that kind of girl. Before the first semester was up, I resigned from the sorority, because I just didn't enjoy it. The sorority was about conformity. I was trying to be a hippie, and those two ideas were not compatible.

Unlike my mother, Josephine Baiamonte, I was Liz Williams, and I soon painfully realized I had some measure of acceptance because of my American-sounding name. When I went to LSU in 1967 I had a friend on my dorm floor who had a very Italian name. On the first day of rush, her assigned freshman roommate wandered down the hall and complained to me that she had an Italian roommate. She didn't know I was also Sicilian. This wasn't the first time in my life I had seen a little of the denigrating attitudes my mother had years ago encountered. But it was one of the most blatant.

My mother admitted that when she got married she went from being Josephine Baiamonte to Jo Williams in less than an hour, and was instantly transformed and sanitized. She did not want me to grow up as a sanitized person, but one aware of her heritage.

INVENTING ITALIAN FOOD IN AMERICA

When it came to American attitudes toward Sicilian food, there was, again, a negative bias. American dieticians and social workers thought Italian immigrants were stubborn for failing to listen to their advice to overcook their pasta to make it more "digestible." They didn't want immigrants to eat many tomatoes because they were too acidic. They thought Italians ate too much cheese, and especially too much garlic, which was déclassé and considered too stimulating. The consumption of spices, seasonings, and wine just added to the list of Italians' dietary sins.

There's been a lot written about Sicilian food's journey to the food Americans think of today as Italian, and history tells us that most Italians ignored attempts at altering their diets, much to the frustration of the well-meaning home economists. In New Orleans, with so many Sicilians living together in the French Quarter, almost from the get-go, Creoles were exposed to authentic Italian and Sicilian food. Known for tossing convention aside, the often-snooty Creoles ate the food of these immigrants in a way that was less acceptable in the rest of the country. For instance, they ate pasta properly, al dente.

The proliferation of spaghetti houses in the French Quarter were, of course, first patronized by the Sicilians. But within ten years of their arrival they were also serving spaghetti to Creoles. To cater to their growing clientele, restaurants expanded their menus by adding the ubiquitous and inexpensive oyster, as well as other local ingredients cooked with a Sicilian twist.

Meanwhile, with Sicilians craving food they recognized, some of them began truck farming in Amite and Tangipahoa Parishes, as well as the Northshore generally. These farmers would bring broccoli, arugula, artichokes, eggplants, garlic, zucchini, and cucuzza back to the city, where many of these vegetables had been unknown. Aside from the Sicilians selling fruits, meat, cheese, and fish in the French Market, their stand-alone grocery stores sold cheeses, salume, canned tomatoes, wines, Italian-style breads, and olives.

Even with attempts to keep food and cooking habits purely Sicilian, in time, traditional Italian tomato sauce turned into New Orleans–style red gravy. Many other special dishes evolved and were adopted by the citizens of New Orleans, such as veal parmesan, oysters and pasta, as well as meatball and Italian sausage po'boys.

A notable Sicilian contribution to sandwich stardom is the muffuletta. Central Grocery was started by Salvatore Lupo on Decatur Street in 1906. Still going strong, the iconic Italian grocer became famous as the home of the muffuletta, a distinctly Sicilian overstuffed sandwich that has entered into the canon of Creole Italian food. The Lupo family touched the heart of New Orleans and created an origin myth for what is known today as the muffuletta. (New Orleanians love a great origin story.) There are several versions of the muffuletta invention, but the most persistent is that wharf workers looking to buy lunch would get muffuletta bread loaves at Central Grocery, along with cold cuts, cheese, and olive salad. Salvatore decided to layer the cold cuts, cheese, and olive salad on the muffuletta loaves ahead of time, thus creating a sandwich that was easier to eat and carry.

Today so many dishes we take for granted, such as Creole barbecued shrimp, owe their origins to Sicilians. But the dishes have been so thoroughly embraced by the people of New Orleans that not only have their origins been forgotten, but the origins really no longer matter.

THE RED BEANS AND RICE BRIDGE

One reason I love red beans and rice is that it's a dish that bridges both worlds, both my New Orleans and Sicilian heritages. I understand red beans and rice, because I understand the dish's association with cooking laundry, which I did with my Nana. And I went to public school and ate in the cafeteria, where we had red beans and rice every Monday, which is a deeply rooted New Orleans tradition.

The usual explanation for eating red beans and rice on Mondays in New Orleans is that Monday is laundry day. A pot of red beans could cook alongside a pot of laundry without much attention, and was a way of using expensive fuel for two purposes instead of one. Today most people use washing machines and do not boil their laundry. But the Monday tradition of red beans and rice persists. The tradition transcends whatever explanation one can give to the origin, and red beans and rice still remains the anticipated Monday special on many restaurant menus.

Mother made red beans and rice regularly. She seasoned hers with ham, which gives an unctuous texture to the beans that sausage simply cannot duplicate. (I think it is the collagen in the ham bone that does it.) Sometimes she served sausage on the side, not cooked in the pot. Sometimes she made a side of fried chicken. Mother always added a bit of oregano to her beans, which tasted garlicky and creamy, and yet still had some chew. I haven't eaten any other red beans like them. Daddy loved red beans and rice, especially because it was served with rice.

Red beans was the one dish that transitioned my mother from the Sicilian table to the New Orleans table. She served this dish from the Creole foreign canon to her mother, who never cooked red beans and rice and who learned from it that my mother had become a different person. That simple dish represented my mother's independence from her family tradition. When my grandparents ate at my parents' house and we had red beans and rice, there was always that unspoken message on that plate.

RED BEANS AND RICE

This recipe doesn't give instructions for soaking the beans overnight, which means you can enjoy the dish the very day you begin cooking. Soaking dried beans does reduce cooking time, but it isn't necessary.

1. Over medium heat, place the bacon fat in a large soup pot with a heavy bottom and sauté the onions until soft and beginning to brown slightly, about 6 minutes. Add the celery and bell pepper and cook another 3 minutes.

2. Add the garlic, bay leaves, paprika, cayenne pepper, thyme, and cloves and stir 1 minute. Add the water and beer and stir well. Bring to a boil, then add the beans and ham bone. After the mixture returns to a boil, reduce the flame to a simmer. Cover the pot and cook 1½ hours.

3. Uncover the pot and cook another hour. Stir occasionally. Taste the beans for salt and adjust for your taste. (Since ham is salty, you might not need more salt.) Stir in the black pepper. Use a fork to mash some of the beans against the side of the pot, mashing just enough beans to make the liquid creamy. Cook another hour, checking for liquid and stirring in more water as necessary. When beans are completely tender and the liquid is thick like gravy, remove the ham bone and serve over rice.

2 tablespoons bacon fat

2 onions, chopped

3 stalks celery, chopped

1 green bell pepper, chopped

3 cloves garlic, minced

3 bay leaves

2 teaspoons sweet paprika

Cayenne pepper to taste

1 teaspoon dried thyme

¼ teaspoon ground cloves

6 cups water

1 (12-ounce) can beer

1 pound dried red beans (also known as red kidney beans)

1 meaty ham bone (if you don't have a ham bone, use 3 or 4 ham hocks)

Salt

2 teaspoons ground black pepper

For serving: 6 cups cooked rice

LASAGNA

This is by no means a traditional recipe for lasagna. But like gumbo, even though everybody's lasagna is different, everyone recognizes it as lasagna. This recipe was always being tweaked by my Nana, my mother, and by me. I do not think anyone would be able to untangle our various contributions. All our versions are over-the-top rich and decadent. I love serving lasagna for Christmas dinner, no matter how untraditional. This is one dish everyone loves regardless of their roots.

When preparing this dish, think generous, that is, use up all of the cheese and sauce. Do not use it sparingly. For parties, it is also wonderful served at room temperature, cut into tiny squares, and placed in mini-cupcake ruffled cups. (If you are going to do this, instead of making two layers of pasta, make only one.)

Olive oil

2 pounds fresh pasta sheets

2 pounds ground beef

2 pounds ground Italian sausage, casings removed

6 cups Nana's Basic Tomato Sauce (recipe page 20)

1 teaspoon cinnamon

2 quarts ricotta cheese

2 large eggs, whisked lightly with a fork

1 cup grated Parmesan cheese, divided

Salt and white pepper to taste

½ pound fresh basil leaves, washed

1 pound shredded mozzarella (not shredded cheese in a bag)

1. Preheat your oven to 350°F. Coat the inside of a deep 9×11-inch roasting pan or casserole with olive oil. Place a layer of fresh pasta in the pan and set aside. (When using fresh pasta there is no need to cook it before.)

2. Coat the inside of a large frying pan with olive oil. Set the pan over medium-high heat and add the ground beef and Italian sausage. Sauté the meat until it is browned, about 10 minutes. Remove the meat from the pan and discard the rendered fat.

3. In a large bowl, mix the tomato sauce with the cinnamon and set it aside. In the bowl of a standing mixer with a paddle attachment, combine the ricotta, eggs, and ½ cup Parmesan. Use medium speed to beat until well blended. Add salt and white pepper.

4. In the roasting pan with the layer of pasta, spread half the ricotta mixture as evenly as possible over the pasta. Add half the meat mixture and spread evenly. Add ⅓ of the tomato sauce and spread evenly. Layer on half of the basil leaves so they lay flat and cover the entire pan. Sprinkle on ⅓ of the shredded mozzarella.

5. Add another layer of pasta, and then the remaining half of the ricotta, the remaining half of the meat mixture, ⅓ of the tomato sauce, the remaining half of the basil leaves, ⅓ of the mozzarella, and a final layer of pasta. Spread on the remaining ⅓ of the tomato sauce. Top with the remaining ⅓ of the shredded mozzarella and the remaining ½ cup Parmesan.

6. Bake uncovered 1 hour. The edges should be briskly bubbling. Remove from the oven and let rest 30 minutes before serving. (This allows the lasagna to firm up. Do not slice it when it first comes out of the oven.) Serve warm.

PASTA ALLA NORMA
(PASTA WITH TOMATO SAUCE AND EGGPLANT)

This dish is named after the heroine of one of Italian composer Vincenzo Salvatore Bellini's most famous operas. It is said that after a group of opera-goers saw the performance they were so bedazzled that they christened anything spectacular as una vera Norma (a real Norma).

1. To make the sauce, place the whole tomatoes and the chopped onion together in a stock pot and cook until the skins of the tomatoes split and they begin to exude their juices, about 30 minutes. Transfer the mixture to a food processor and process into a rough sauce. Return the sauce to the pot and add salt. Continue cooking 1½ hours, with the lid of the pot ajar to allow steam and evaporation. Add the ½ cup basil leaves and stir. Place the lid on tightly and turn off the heat.

2. Add oil to a heavy pot set over medium-high heat. While oil is heating, peel and cube the eggplant. The oil is ready when a pinch of flour sizzles when dropped in. Fry the eggplant in batches until the cubes are soft on the inside and crispy on the outside, about 10 minutes. Remove the eggplant to a plate and lightly salt each batch. Return any pooled oil back to the pot.

3. Boil the pasta according to package directions. Drain the pasta and stir in the tomato sauce and eggplant. Arrange on a large platter and garnish with the ricotta salata and fresh basil leaves.

6 pounds fresh Roma tomatoes

3 cups chopped cippolini or other sweet onion (Vidalias are a good substitute)

1 teaspoon salt

½ cup fresh basil leaves, packed, plus more for serving

3 cups peanut oil or canola oil

3 pounds eggplant

Sea salt to taste

Water for boiling

2 packages penne rigate or other small tube-shaped pasta

For serving: 1½ ounces ricotta salata, grated

PASTA CON BROCCOLI E ALICI
(PASTA WITH BROCCOLI AND ANCHOVIES)

MAKES 4 SERVINGS

This dish is the reason I love anchovies, and it's full of flavor without costing lots of money. When growing up, my family particularly enjoyed this dish after we'd been out and came home starving. Whoever was cooking had to rely on what was in the pantry, which always had cans of anchovies, cheese, and pasta. If we were out of farfalle, we would use something else. I used to think the casual way Sicilians cooked—substituting freely, omitting things, and just making do—was what made them so easygoing. Now I know I had it backward. They took care with ingredients, but the rule was to use good ingredients, not to be obsessive about recipes. That is a good way to live life in general.

1. Bring a big pot of salted water to a boil and add the farfalle. After the water comes back to a boil, add the broccoli florets and cubes to the same pot. Boil until the pasta is cooked.

2. While the pasta is cooking, in a large, deep skillet set over medium-high heat, add the olive oil and mix in the anchovies and garlic. Cook and stir until the anchovies have dissolved into the oil.

3. Dip out a cup of water from the pasta pot, then drain the pasta and broccoli. Add the pasta to the skillet and stir it with the oil and anchovy mixture, tossing to coat. Add the chili flakes, salt, pepper, and Parmesan. If it seems too dry, add a few tablespoons of the pasta water. Serve in bowls, with Parmesan passed at the table.

Water for boiling

Salt and pepper

1 pound farfalle

2½ pounds broccoli, cut into florets and stems peeled and cut into cubes

3 tablespoons olive oil

3 ounces anchovies

3 cloves garlic, minced

Dried chili flakes to taste

½ cup grated Parmesan, plus more for the table

ORECCHIETTE IN BRODO ("SMALL EAR" PASTA IN BROTH)

MAKES 4 SERVINGS

1. Combine the 2 flours into a little mountain on your countertop. Punch a crater into the top of the mountain. Pour half the water into the crater. Use a fork to pull the sides of the crater into the water and mix until the flour is all incorporated.

2. Flour your hands and knead the dough until it becomes smooth and pliable. Roll it into logs about ½ inch thick. Cut the dough logs into ½-inch pieces. Roll each piece into a ball the size of a large pea. Press one side of each ball with your other thumb to flatten it. The resulting shape should resemble an ear. Repeat with all the dough balls.

3. Bring the broth to a simmer in a pot. Drop the little ears of pasta into the broth and bring the broth back up to a simmer. The ears are ready when they float to the top. If you decide not to use all the pasta, it can be refrigerated or frozen in a resealable plastic bag and saved for later. Ladle the pasta and broth into soup bowls and let each person garnish with olive oil, gremolata, and Parmesan cheese.

1 cup semolina flour

1 cup unbleached all-purpose flour

½–⅔ cup water

2 quarts good, rich chicken or beef broth

For serving: olive oil, Gremolata (recipe page 14), and grated Parmesan cheese

PIMENTO CHEESE PASTA

MAKES 4 SERVINGS

My American father fit in well with my mother's family full of Sicilians. He laughed easily and loved having a good time. He was pretty laid back about the food, too, and he appreciated that Italian food was delicious. However, there were certain dishes he couldn't give up from his childhood. One of them was pimento cheese. Since my mother loved him, she created this mash-up of one of his favorite comfort foods and one of hers.

Water for boiling

1 pound rigatoni

2 cups Pimento Cheese (recipe page 19), at room temperature

1 cup coarsely chopped raw celery

¼ cup chopped fresh parsley

2 slices crumbled bacon

1 teaspoon smoked paprika

1. Cook the rigatoni in boiling water according to package directions. Reserve a cup of pasta cooking water, then drain the pasta.

2. Mix the pimento cheese and the chopped celery into the pasta. Use a bit of the cooking water to loosen it up if needed. Place on a platter and sprinkle on the parsley, bacon, and paprika. Serve immediately.

QUICK TOMATO SAUCE

MAKES 4 SERVINGS

When making pasta sauce with vine-ripened tomatoes, there is no need to cook it for hours. Let the fresh taste of the tomatoes leap out.

1. Heat the olive oil in a sauté pan until it's hot. Add the diced onions and slowly cook them until they are slightly browned, about 8 minutes. Add the garlic to the pan and cook 2 minutes. Add the tomatoes and cook until they're soft, stirring occasionally, for 30 minutes. If the tomatoes become too dry, add up to ½ cup of red wine.

2. When the tomatoes are soft, add the lemon and orange zests. Add salt and pepper to taste. For a traditional way to serve, toss the sauce with hot pasta and basil leaves. Serve immediately. Pass grated Parmesan cheese at the table.

¼ cup olive oil

1 medium onion, cut to a medium dice

2 cloves garlic, minced

1 pound unpeeled fresh tomatoes (If the tomatoes are large, chop them into a medium dice. If they are cherry tomatoes, slice them in half.)

½ cup red wine (optional)

1 teaspoon lemon zest

1 teaspoon orange zest

Salt and pepper

For serving: 8 ounces cooked pasta, ¼ cup fresh, torn basil leaves, and grated Parmesan cheese

BUTTERNUT SQUASH SAUCE FOR PASTA

MAKES 4 TO 6 SERVINGS

Sometimes you want pasta and not tomato sauce. This is especially true in winter, when tomatoes are out of season and there is an abundance of butternut squash. Of course, the quick solution is to make pasta with garlic, olive oil, and cheese. There's nothing wrong with that. But when you want a richer sauce, butternut squash is perfect.

1 medium butternut squash

3 tablespoons olive oil, plus more for oiling the squash

5 cloves garlic, minced

1 cup white wine

1 tablespoon minced fresh sage leaves, plus additional whole leaves for frying

Salt and pepper to taste

For serving: cooked pasta and grated Parmesan cheese

1. Preheat your oven to 325°F. Cut the squash in half lengthwise. Scoop out the seeds and discard them. Oil the cut sides of the squash and place them cut side down on a sheet pan. Bake until tender, about 1 hour.

2. Remove the baked squash from the oven and scoop out the pulp with a spoon. Heat a skillet with the 3 tablespoons olive oil. Add the squash pulp and the garlic and stir, using dribbles of the wine to loosen the sauce. Cook 20 minutes, watching carefully, because the sauce has a tendency to stick to the pan.

3. Add the sage and salt and pepper. If desired, heat a little olive oil in a small skillet and quickly fry a handful of whole sage leaves. Toss the sauce with hot pasta and garnish with the fried sage leaves. Pass the grated cheese at the table.

GRITS

MAKES 4 SERVINGS

Another dish my father loved was polenta, which is often used interchangeably with grits, but which my family definitely knew was different from grits. Grits today are usually mass-produced using white corn. Polenta is made with yellow corn and has a coarser grind than modern grits. But stone-ground yellow grits, the kind my family bought when we ate grits, are much like polenta. And if we were out of one, we used the other—different but the same.

Although corn polenta is not traditional in Sicily, polenta made with other forms of grain has been commonly eaten there since Roman times. So when Sicilians arrived in New Orleans, they naturally gravitated to using local and inexpensive corn grits. Grits were yet another thing that Sicily and the American South, especially Louisiana, had in common. Both populations worked the fields, and poverty sometimes forced them to exist on vegetables. They also loved tomatoes, music, and a good time. And in Louisiana we eat grits.

Corn is inexpensive, and so are beans. When combined they make a complete protein, so even those who could not afford meat, such as the early Sicilian immigrants, could eat corn (in the form of grits) and beans for a good source of protein.

As the early twentieth-century lovers of ground corn became more prosperous, whether American or Sicilian, instead of abandoning ground corn for something more exotic, they simply gussied up their ground corn. In Louisiana we add butter, cream, cheese, and other good things to our grits, both at home and in restaurants. Polenta in Italy is often enriched with the same luscious fats. We have to admit that plain grits are good too. Grits also make a good starch base for other dishes, such as grillades and grits, one of my father's favorites. And grits, of course, are great for breakfast. To make a complete meal, just top your bowl with an egg with a runny yolk.

My father was also always up for chicken cacciatore served with polenta. When we made actual polenta, we bought Italian imports from

8 cups water

2 teaspoons salt

2 cups grits

For serving: 1 tablespoon olive oil (optional)

Solari's or Central Grocery. We often fried leftover polenta, which is nothing more than cold, hardened polenta fried in olive oil until it's crispy on the outside and creamy in the middle. Sometimes this tasted better than the original dish.

In a large pot, boil the water and salt. While whisking, slowly add the grits. When it comes to a boil, lower to a simmer and cook 30 minutes, whisking constantly. Serve grits hot.

After they're cooked you can add anything you want, but the luscious corn flavor can be masked by pouring in lots of cream or cheese. If you have good stone-ground grits, only a tablespoon of olive oil is necessary.

SPRING RISOTTO

MAKES 6 SERVINGS

This is one of those very Italian dishes that is more about method than particular ingredients. You make risotto with rice and whatever vegetables are fresh from your garden or the market. The ingredients below are mostly suggestions, so if you do not have peas, just use something else fresh, or use more leeks or asparagus. For this version of risotto, the most essential vegetable is the asparagus, but it is delicious even without that. My Nana liked to display her cosmopolitan nature by cooking risotto.

2 tablespoons olive oil

1 tablespoon butter

2 leeks, the white parts and the light green tender parts, cleaned and sliced

1 cup chopped fennel bulb

1½ cups Arborio rice

1 cup dry white wine

4 to 5 cups broth, simmering

1 pound spring asparagus, trimmed into 2-inch pieces

1½ cups fresh shelled peas

Zest of 2 lemons

2 tablespoons lemon juice

1 cup grated Parmesan cheese

Salt and pepper to taste

For serving: ½ cup chopped fresh mint

1. Add the oil and butter to a sauté pan and sauté the leeks and fennel until they are just cooked, about 10 minutes. Add the rice and coat it thoroughly with the oil. Add the wine and bring to a simmer. Stir to encourage the starches to combine with the liquid. Cook until the wine has been absorbed by the rice, about 15 minutes.

2. Ladle in 2 cups of the simmering broth. Stir often to encourage the starchy creaminess to develop. After about 20 minutes, add the asparagus and peas. Continue to stir, and as the liquid is absorbed keep adding ladles of broth. After about 20 more minutes, the rice should be tender, but not mushy.

3. Remove the pan from the heat. Stir in the lemon zest and lemon juice, and then the Parmesan cheese. Taste for saltiness, then adjust the salt and add pepper. (If you want your risotto a bit more creamy, add 2 tablespoons cream, but I think this step reduces the flavor of the vegetables and is unnecessary.) Spoon onto a platter and serve warm topped with fresh mint.

JAMBALAYA

My totally American father loved rice, his starch of choice. Since he was a native of Louisiana, he felt that eating rice, an important commercial crop of this state, was a birthright. He probably didn't know that an Italian named Angelo Socolo at one time had been Louisiana's largest rice farmer. Had he known, he would have argued that my mother should make rice more often.

My father loved that Cajun favorite, rice and gravy. He also often lobbied for jambalaya. My mother always made her jambalaya with leftover rice, which she often made too much of intentionally when she made gumbo.

A big reason she used leftover rice was that she hated gummy rice, so she never made jambalaya from scratch the way we do today. Instead she'd use her firmer leftover cooked rice, which she felt gave her more control. She'd add chopped or shredded chicken, leftover ham, sausage, and seafood, usually shrimp. The dribs and drabs of things leftover in the refrigerator often wandered into the jambalaya, and it was different every time. Using up leftovers was part of the New Orleans canon. And my mother, with one foot in Sicily and one foot in New Orleans, knew exactly how the finished dish should taste. Jambalaya was one of the few dishes she did not embellish with basil or oregano.

3 tablespoons oil (canola oil, olive oil, bacon fat, or duck fat)

2 medium onions, chopped

1 green bell pepper, chopped

3 or 4 stalks celery, chopped

3 cloves garlic, minced

Meat from 1 cooked chicken, removed from the bone, chopped or shredded

3 pounds smoked andouille sausage, cut into coins about ½ inch thick

4 or 5 fresh tomatoes, chopped, with the juice (enough to make 3 cups total)

2 pounds shrimp, peeled and deveined

3 or 4 teaspoons ground cayenne pepper

1 tablespoon paprika

1 tablespoon salt (see note below)

1 tablespoon ground black pepper

1 teaspoon dried thyme

3 bay leaves

6 cups cooked rice

About a cup of chicken broth (if needed)

1 bunch parsley, chopped

1. Heat the oil in a large, heavy-bottomed pot. Sauté the onions, bell pepper, celery, and garlic until soft, about 5 minutes. Add chicken and sausage and simmer briskly, stirring constantly, for 5 minutes.

2. Mix in the tomatoes and juice. Stir in the spices and the bay leaves. Add the rice. Mix until everything is evenly distributed. Bring the liquid to a boil, then turn off the burner and add the shrimp. (If the shrimp are already cooked, allow them to come to room temperature and toss with the rice mixture right before serving.) Stir the mixture and cover. Let it sit untouched until the rice absorbs the liquid and the shrimp are cooked, about 10 minutes. Serve the jambalaya warm.

NOTE: Both andouille and shrimp add salt, so if you do not want your food over-salted, wait 10 minutes before serving to add salt.

CHAPTER 4

CLINGING TO SICILIAN ROOTS

Soups

Sali mitticcinnee navisazzo, conzola quantu vua . . . ma sempre è cucuzza.
(You may garnish it with as much salt and pepper as you want, but pumpkin still has little flavor.)
—Sicilian proverb

The Sicilians who migrated to New Orleans had not been eating pasta and cheese daily back in Sicily. What they probably ate was bread, and maybe cornmeal. They might have foraged for dandelions or other plants in season. Even if they had produced their own good crops, peasants in Sicily did not eat well.

In New Orleans, the new immigrants joyously found abundant food that was affordable and available. They even had the opportunity to own the source of much of their food, their own farmland, upon which they could grow crops and sell the excess. And as they sold from vegetable, fruit, and prepared-food carts, and from their market stalls, grocery stores, bars, and restaurants, they established themselves and exposed local, eager New Orleanians to new Sicilian flavors.

Through all their trials and errors, these Sicilians tried to preserve their country's food traditions. Tradition is important, and we must recognize that traditions constantly change, sometimes intentionally and sometimes inadvertently. The food of New Orleans, for example, clearly and steadily transforms with new immigrants, new American trends, and new generations. I have seen my family traditions change with time, and I have seen my personal hold on them loosen. Growing up with both Italian and New Orleans food traditions, both central to my identity, I have found it impossible not to meld them together. Sometimes those traditions remained pure, but often I mixed them together out of necessity and convenience.

I was born in 1950, and by the time I was old

enough to remember things, the Sicilian-speaking community was shrinking. When I was very young, our family would attend social events where the language of Sicily was spoken, where the food of Sicily was eaten, and where the music of Sicily was played. By the time I was a teenager, there were few people left who spoke the Sicilian dialect. We no longer played the instruments and sang songs that reflected the island. Those Old World tunes were replaced by Perry Como, Frank Sinatra, Dean Martin, and New Orleans–born Louis Prima. The actual immigrants with roots in Sicily itself had passed on, and all that was left that could be considered Sicilian were food traditions.

A LESSON ON OYSTERS

A strong Sicilian tradition was a love of oysters. Many immigrant Sicilians in New Orleans who worked in the outdoor markets sold oysters by the sack. Although oysters are not a regular part of the Sicilian diet, mussels are, and eating various types of clams is well established along the entire Sicilian coast.

That immigrant Sicilian reverence of oysters has continued through the generations. When I was six or seven years old, for one of our many family gatherings my Papa ordered a half sack of oysters. While the other adults drank beer and talked, he pulled out a table and an asbestos roof-tile ridge cap. The roof tile made a snug, stable holder for the unshucked oysters, and he used his oyster knife to pry their ridged shells open.

He was soon joined by my oyster-loving father, Grover Cleveland Williams Jr., known by his family as June, short for Junior, and by everyone else as Cleve. Unlike my mother, he was tall, about six feet. I'd always been told that in his young days he had thick brown hair, but I only remember him virtually bald. After the popular *Kojak* TV detective show aired in the 1970s, he

Papa after shucking oysters

began shaving his head, he said to save barber money. He also had beautiful teeth and a winning smile, and was the person who laughed so loud and infectiously in the theater that people would seek him out after the play. My fondest memory of him was of that laugh, and the way he tickled and teased and knew how to play.

My grandfather, Frank, and my father, Cleve, were the best of friends, and Cleve actually became the son Frank never had. The two bought a boat together and a fishing camp, and they spent lots of time fishing and crabbing. Together they invested in the stock market and ran my grandfather's export-forwarding business, Trans Marine, which Papa started and then sold to Cleve. (My mother never forgave my Papa for not put-

Papa in 1930

and letting the oyster slip down your throat. The oyster looked like raw ones always do, slimy, but I was too proud to hesitate and so mentally prepared myself to swallow this weird, unknown thing. I let the oyster slip down my throat, and surprisingly judged this a delicious treat. I held out my hand for more, and I was roundly praised for being sophisticated enough to appreciate raw oysters. I was patted on the back, and other adults came over to watch me eat them. I felt very grown-up. My family's love of oysters is still going strong, and I have taught my children to eat raw oysters, too.

FOOD CARTS

A thriving street food scene in early twentieth-century New Orleans contained its share of Sicilians, who mainly pushed carts piled with fruits and vegetables. When vendors saved enough, they often upgraded to horse- or mule-drawn wagons.

Roman Candy. The mule-drawn Roman Candy cart that sold candy over one hundred years ago still rolls through the streets of the city, complete with a mule. Sales began in 1915, when Sam Cortese, the grandfather of today's Roman Candyman, sold his Italian mother's leftover taffy on his vegetable cart. Sam was a street vendor from childhood, leaving school after a serious streetcar accident left him disabled. His mother, Angelina Napoli Cortese, was known for the flavorful taffy she made for special events, and Sam thought there would be a constant demand for it. Unfortunately, she was too busy to produce the candy in the quantity he needed, so he began exploring the means to make and sell the candy all the time. He designed a cart that allowed him to make and pull the candy as the mule pulled it down the street.

Sam Cortese and Tom Brinker, a wheelwright,

ting the business in her name, but Papa wanted his business owned by a man.)

My father was born in 1918 in the small, landlocked northwest Louisiana town of Harmon, and was therefore not a fan of seafood. But he really, really loved raw oysters, and at this particular party I was at the age when children were typically introduced to them. I had always watched adults eat those slimy gray bivalves straight out the shell, and I loved fried oysters, but I had never tried one raw.

My father and my Papa called me over and handed me a rather small half shell with an oyster on it. My father also had one, and so did Papa. They encouraged me to eat by demonstrating the technique of holding one side of the shell against your lip, tipping up the shell, outfitted the wagon in 1915, and since then it hasn't changed much. Sam died in 1969, and his grandson, Ron Kottemann, took over the job of making and selling the candy from the cart. Cortese and Kottemann are the only two family members who have regularly driven it. Today, Kottemann sells chocolate, strawberry, and vanilla taffy. Each stick is hand-wrapped in waxed paper.

As a testament to the staying power of Roman Candy, the three flavors are featured in rums produced and sold by a local spirits company called Roman Candy Rum.

Waffles. Although they are no longer in service, wagons similar to the Roman Candy cart sold waffles, and they were often driven and owned by Sicilians. Louis Gandolini sold waffles from a cart from 1916 to 1958. His prices went from six waffles for five cents when he started to four waffles for five cents when he retired. Gandolini's waffles were hot and covered with powdered sugar. According to Howard Jacobs in the *Times-Picayune,* he was said to be the last of the "wafflemen." Gandolini tried to sell his waffle iron to the Roman Candy owner, Sam Cortese, but Cortese wasn't interested.

Although the waffle was not a Sicilian invention, I certainly remember loving them. Fortunately for my waistline, we lived in Lakeview, which was not convenient to the places the waffle wagon was parked. But when there was reason to pass the waffle wagon, my mother, who loved the waffles too, would always stop. We would share an order, with powdered sugar dusting our clothes. I still prefer waffles with powdered sugar rather than syrup.

Lucky Dogs. A famous food cart, actually now a fleet of carts, is the one that sells Lucky Dog hotdogs. The first Lucky Dog cart was originally peddled on the street by Steve and Erasmus Loyacano (originally Loiacano). The brothers were of Sicilian descent, and they founded the company in 1947, which was eleven years after the Oscar Mayer cart made its debut in 1936. Lucky Dog carts differed from Oscar Mayer's in that they were and still are actual food carts, not merely a marketing vehicle. The Lucky Dog company was sold in 1970 to Doug Talbot and Peter Briant. The corporation is still going strong, with its highly recognizable red and yellow umbrella-topped carts shaped like giant hot dogs. The carts sell from designated spots in the French Quarter, and vendors actually cook the hot dogs on the street.

Snoballs. Snoballs are arguably related to an Italian practice credited to the Emperor Nero. A couple of thousand years ago, during hot months Nero was said to have his minions collect ice from the mountains. The refreshing snow was mixed with fruit and syrups to create a special treat.

Although New Orleans does not have mountains, by the nineteenth century it had ice manufacturing. The Sicilians who came here in the last part of that century were familiar with the practice of flavoring snow and of making homemade syrups. George Ortolano, a first-generation child of Sicilian immigrants, decided to add snoballs to his offerings at his grocery store. At this time, New Orleans snoballs were made with ice shaved by a hand plane that produced a fluffy "snow" that was sweetened with syrup. In 1936, Ortolano created a machine that shaved the ice, making the process much easier and quicker. Ortolano's interest then shifted from selling snoballs to manufacturing the machines that made the snow. He called his invention the Snow-Wizard Snowball Machine. Ultimately, he renamed the machine the SnoWizard Snoball Machine. By commercially manufacturing the machine,

Ortolano made it possible for anyone who could afford a machine to open a snoball stand. Currently Ronnie Sciortino, Ortolano's nephew, runs the company.

Every neighborhood used to have a snoball stand that would open when school let out for summer. As a youngster, I would save my pennies to ride my bike to the snoball stand on Harrison Avenue. This was the time before snoballs were gilded with pineapple, condensed milk (although I do remember an evaporated-milk option), cherries, or ice cream. Today, snoball stands are not as numerous, but there are still plenty of them around the city.

MACARONI FACTORIES AND SPAGHETTI HOUSES

Whether to fulfill a dream of having access to pasta or because it was just good business sense, the Sicilians who settled in the French Quarter created an epicenter of what were called macaroni factories. Probably first established in the late nineteenth century, by the second decade of the twentieth century, these pasta manufacturers were a thriving center of commerce. According to Justin A. Nystrom in *Creole Italian: Sicilian Immigrants and the Shaping of New Orleans Food Culture,* there were eight macaroni factories in the first decade of the 1900s, seven in the French Quarter and six owned by Sicilians. There certainly may have been an unlicensed cottage industry of pasta makers, but that is not documented. The licensed market thrived with only a small markup, and was especially helped by the Dingley Tariff Act in 1897, which doubled the price of imported pasta and made local production more attractive.

Giacomo Cusimano, after operating a small factory, built a large macaroni factory. A non-Sicilian employee from Cusimano's factory, Leon Tujaque, saw his suc-

cess and with non-Sicilian partners opened his own macaroni factory. Tujaque called his new venture the Southern Macaroni Company. Its product, Luxury Brand pasta, is still sold in America today.

Cusimano had had the reputation of helping other Sicilians get started in business. He is said to have financially helped Giuseppe Uddo, who opened the company that eventually grew into Progresso Foods. Many Sicilian food companies started in New Orleans and grew into national prominence. But like Luxury Brand and Progresso Foods, in the mind of the American public they have lost their ties to New Orleans.

With so many Sicilians living in the French Quarter and laboring on the Mississippi River, it stands to reason that places that served quick and inexpensive meals of pasta—often with tomato sauce—proliferated. The local pasta factories cranked out volumes, and Sicilians who knew how to cook pasta and, more importantly, not overcook it, prepared it for those who took comfort in eating it. A few examples of early twentieth-century spaghetti houses were Messina's, Pascal's Manale, and LaNasa's. As time went on, these restaurants also served New Orleans Creole favorites, such as oyster dishes and fresh local fish. Over the years, Messina's and Pascal's Manale have evolved greatly, and are today considered iconic Creole Italian restaurants. LaNasa's has long closed.

The many Sicilian musicians in the city benefitted from spaghetti houses as, along with African Americans, they played jazz for diners. Aside from entertainment, many spaghetti-house patrons expected wine to be part of the meal. Like the rest of the culinary scene in New Orleans, drinking alcohol was considered a regular part of life and culture. It is rumored that even during Prohibition wine and other drinking continued in New Orleans spaghetti houses.

Not every Creole Italian eating establishment in

the city was Sicilian. The most notable example was the more ostentatious Turci's, which was started by husband-and-wife opera singers who moved to New Orleans, one from Bologna and one from Naples. The couple opened a restaurant next to the already famous Begue's Exchange, which later became Tujague's. Later they moved their restaurant to Bourbon Street and then to Poydras Street. The owners were well-traveled and created a fine dining establishment, as opposed to the more café-like spaghetti house. Turci's served New Orleans favorites, and it also offered Creole Italian foods brought to the white-tablecloth level. It operated until the mid-twentieth century.

SOLARI'S GROCERY

Solari's Grocery opened in 1864 on Royal Street. The store's original owner was J. B. Solari, who was not Sicilian, but from Genoa, and he had a European understanding of what immigrants wanted to buy, as well as what locals needed. Solari's stayed open until 1964, and it was popular the whole time it was in business.

One unique feature, for New Orleans, was that the store printed a catalog that customers could pick up or receive by mail. Solari's had a large mail-order service and shipped products all over the country. They also took local orders by telephone and had extensive delivery services. The Southern Food & Beverage Museum has one of Solari's wooden delivery boxes, which fits into a rack on the back of a bicycle. The box is stackable, making it easy to stack several.

In the 1920s the Solari family sold the store, and the new owners ordered a renovation. When it reopened it boasted a dining counter and a food department that served already prepared dishes to take home to warm up and serve—quite an innovation at the time. Maybe this is one reason why, in the mid-twentieth

century, Clementine Paddleford wrote in *Gourmet* magazine that Solari's was one of America's best groceries.

I remember childhood excursions by bus and streetcar to Solari's, which was exciting, mainly because of the store's numerous sights and smells. Some patrons spoke Italian. The store was always crowded, and having children underfoot wasn't conducive to pleasant shopping. When my mother, grandmother, and I visited, I'd be plopped up on a stool to keep me out of the way and safe. I always wanted a stool by the candy counter, where confectioners kneaded marzipan, then shaped it into fruits and whatnots and painted them with food coloring. I was polite and behaved well enough so that I was often rewarded with tiny pinches of marzipan. Because the marzipan artisans knew my grandmother, while I waited for her to finish shopping, often they'd give me a tiny sandwich to eat, usually gorgonzola sometimes dotted with black olives, sautéed eggplant, or thinly sliced tomatoes.

And I remember so much salumi! I would tell my grandmother what I would want for the week—mortadella, ham, and salami. The clerks would hold up paper thin slices of meat, "Like this?" Nana would nod her approval.

After Solari's we often walked to Decatur Street to one of the other Italian groceries like Central or Progressive. There my grandmother would buy olives, mushrooms, nuts, and spices. These stores were not as fancy as Solari's, and there I was not treated like a little doll.

After a trip to the Italian grocers, our packages always smelled so good on the ride home on the streetcar or the bus. Those memories are strong.

BAKERIES

When the French established New Orleans in 1718, the first bakeries, naturally, were run by the French. But the style of bread and majority of bakery ownerships changed dramatically when the Sicilians moved in. Here are a few of their most enduring:

Brocato's. Angelo Brocato Sr. opened a bakery and gelateria in the French Quarter in 1905, after having apprenticed at an established gelateria and bakery in Palermo. He catered to Sicilian tastes and traditions with such sweets as *torroncino* (Italian nougat), *granite al limone* (lemon granita), and all types of cannoli. He later expanded within the French Quarter to a shop that allowed him to re-create the style of gelateria he knew from Palermo. After Angelo Sr.'s death, his sons, Angelo Jr. and Joseph, continued with the traditions.

As time and tastes changed, this highly popular sweet shop had to adapt. In particular, as Sicilians began moving out of the French Quarter, Brocato's found itself losing its major customer base. When home freezers became available, ice-cream lovers started making their own. To keep up with new traditions, Brocato's began producing and packing food for sale to groceries. In 1981 Brocato's moved out of the French Quarter to their current retail store on North Carrollton, which they opened in 1978, and which allowed their expanded business to flourish. The company continues with brisk in-store sales, and it also does a healthy business selling ices and cookies to grocery retailers.

John Gendusa Bakery. John Gendusa arrived in New Orleans from Sicily, and in 1922 he opened a bakery to do what so many others did: he adapted what he knew to what was needed. Italy's bread recipes had to be altered in New Orleans, because of the water, the flour available, and the yeast, as well as a different geography and different tastes and demands. For example, the Martin brothers of the Martin Brothers Restaurant developed the po'boy sandwich, and they turned to Gendusa to come up with a long loaf of bread uniform in size from end to end, which resulted in little bread waste. Gendusa's Bakery also produced round muffuletta loaves for the now famous sandwiches.

United Bakery. In the late 1800s, Sicilian Giuseppe Ruffino opened Ruffino's Bakery on St. Philip Street in the French Quarter. In 1913 Giuseppe sold an interest in the bakery to his son-in-law, Nicolo Evola, who operated under the name Evola Bakery on Royal Street, and later opened United Bakery on St. Bernard Avenue. The tradition was carried on by Nicolo's son, Dominick, and later Dominick's son, Sal Logiudice.

My family often bought bread from United Bakery. We knew that Central Grocery bought their muffuletta loaves from United, and we bought the bakery's plaited loaves that broke apart in just a special way. The crust was hard, but it was not tough, and the inside was chewy. This bread was perfect for eating with Creole cream cheese and fresh figs in the mornings, or for dipping in tomato sauce. My favorite snack was this crispy bread with a dollop of Creole cream cheese topped with Lemon Ice.

United continued in the good hands of the family, operated by descendants, until 2005, when floodwaters from Hurricane Katrina ruined the building and the bakery's original clay ovens suffered irreparable damage.

COLD SAFFRON SOUP

When my two sons were small and interested in all things adult, my husband and I bought them black T-shirts silk-screened to look like the front of a tuxedo. For dinner parties we often gave each son a towel to drape over his arm, and we coached them in asking about drinks: "May I get you a drink? What would you like?" Then the kids brought food to the table and cleared.

The children loved participating in adult events, and they loved the attention and approval they received from our dinner guests. Most of all, they learned about expected behavior at something other than a chaotic family event. They saw that manners were real and not torture imposed by parents, and they learned about the art of sharing meals and making things special for friends. They grew interested in serving pieces, table decorations, and things to which children are often oblivious. This exercise prompted them to invite their young friends for dinner, as well as adults they wanted to impress, acquaintances such as teachers and camp counselors. We allowed them to invite their adult guests to dinner. Multigenerational friendships are wonderful things.

When we included our children as helpers, we had to serve food they could handle without spilling, dropping, or injuring anyone. Usually that meant cold soup, not hot, and usually salad. We never prepared anything too messy, and we always had them help out in the kitchen. My children often served this cold soup, which was simple yet special, and good for summer suppers.

2 quarts unsalted chicken stock

4 or 5 small leeks, washed well

3 medium carrots

2 small white potatoes

3 tablespoons chopped shallot

A large pinch of saffron

2 cups buttermilk

1 cup dry white wine

Juice of half a lemon

Salt and pepper to taste

For serving: chopped parsley or chives

1. Bring the stock to a boil in a large pot. Meanwhile, rough chop the leeks, carrots, and potatoes. Add the vegetables, shallot and saffron to the stock and simmer until the vegetables are tender, about 30 minutes. Set aside to cool.

2. Purée the vegetables and the stock until smooth in a food processor or with a stick blender. Refrigerate the mixture. When ready to serve, stir in the buttermilk, wine, and lemon juice. Adjust the seasoning with the salt and pepper. Serve in chilled bowls garnished with chopped parsley or chives.

BROCCOLI SOUP

MAKES 6 SERVINGS

My mother always peeled broccoli stems, chopped the tender parts, and tossed them into this soup with the florets. Nothing was wasted. And when we had leftover cauliflower, she would add it to the soup for a broccoli and cauliflower version, which was my favorite.

This is a forgiving soup, and you can experiment by adding things like leftover broccoli rabe or spinach. This particular version is more sumptuous than an original Sicilian version, which would have used water instead of stock. To make it even more decadent, when cooking the broccoli add a piece of Parmesan rind, and remove it before serving.

1. Bring the stock to a simmer and add the broccoli, tomatoes, garlic, oregano, and bay leaves. Cook, uncovered, until the broccoli is just tender, about 5 minutes.

2. Add the pasta and cook according to package directions until just al dente. Cooking time will depend on the shape of the pasta. Remove the pot from the heat. Just before serving, add the basil leaves. Adjust for salt and pepper. Ladle the hot soup into large bowls. At the table, garnish with Parmesan cheese and olive oil and serve with a side of bread.

3 quarts chicken stock

4 cups broccoli florets, chopped small enough to eat with a soup spoon

1 (14.5-ounce) can San Marzano tomatoes, diced, with liquid

4 cloves garlic, minced

2 tablespoons dried oregano

2 bay leaves

½ pound pasta (not a long pasta)

1 cup fresh basil leaves

Salt and pepper to taste

For serving: grated Parmesan cheese, olive oil, and crusty bread

OYSTERS IN TOMATO BISQUE

MAKES 4 SERVINGS

Combine the tomato sauce and buttermilk in a large saucepan set over medium heat. Stir often and cook until the mixture simmers. Add the oysters and their liquor and continue cooking until the bisque simmers again. Cook until the oysters begin to curl, but no longer than 10 minutes. Serve hot in bowls. Top with parsley and sides of crusty bread for dipping.

4 cups Nana's Basic Tomato Sauce (recipe page 20)

1 cup buttermilk

1 pint fresh oysters, with the liquor

For serving: ½ cup chopped, fresh flat-leaf parsley and crusty French bread

ROASTED TOMATO SOUP

I tend to save bits of cheese that have gotten hard. This would be the time to throw those pieces of cheese into the food processor along with the tomatoes and make them part of this soup. Also, don't use Roma tomatoes for this recipe; you want tomatoes that are really juicy.

1. Preheat oven to 400°F. Remove stems from tomatoes and rub the tomatoes with olive oil. Rub the onion and the garlic cloves with olive oil. Wrap the garlic in aluminum foil. Place the garlic packet and the tomatoes, onion, and sun-dried tomato halves on a cookie sheet. Bake 1 hour.

2. Remove the roasted vegetables from the oven, place in a food processor with the oregano, and process until the mixture is uniform. Add any juices and oil left at the bottom of the cookie sheet.

3. Place the tomato mixture in a pot with the broth, wine, and goat cheese. Mix well and simmer over low heat, uncovered, for 30 minutes. The cheese should be fully incorporated. Check for seasoning, adding salt and pepper to taste. Serve hot, garnished with a good olive oil and chopped black olives.

7 or 8 large tomatoes

Olive oil

1 medium onion, peeled and quartered

5 whole cloves garlic, peeled

7 or 8 sun-dried tomato halves packed in oil

¼ cup fresh oregano leaves

2 cups chicken broth

2 cups dry white wine

4 ounces goat cheese

Salt and pepper

For serving: olive oil and chopped black olives

TURKEY BONE GUMBO

MAKES 8 TO 12 SERVINGS

For my taste there is only one reason to eat turkey on Thanksgiving, and that is the opportunity to have a turkey carcass and leftovers for making Turkey Bone Gumbo. I always make too much gravy, vegetables, and dressing so that I'll have leftovers for gumbo. Even if the gravy contains mushrooms and other vegetables, as mine does, add it all. (I almost always put mushrooms in my turkey gravy.) In the roasting pan, my turkey sits on a bed of carrots. Although everyone eats these carrots at the Thanksgiving meal, there are usually some left over, and they, too, go into the gumbo pot. And if I have peas in roux, I put them in the pot also.

For Thanksgiving, I always make a cornbread and oyster dressing. Sometimes I also add crawfish. Instead of serving my Turkey Bone Gumbo with rice, I plop a large dollop of this dressing into the bowl of gumbo, as the Cajuns do with potato salad.

In anticipation of the filé I serve as a condiment with my gumbo, I usually baste the turkey with at least one bottle of root beer, which has a similar taste to sassafras, the leaf that is ground up to make filé. This not only helps impart a beautiful color to the turkey's skin, but adds a sweet richness to the gravy and drippings. In turn the root beer adds a haunting sweetness to the gumbo, which has a hint of sassafras when sprinkled with filé at the table.

¼ cup all-purpose flour

¼ vegetable oil or bacon fat, or even duck fat, if you have it

2 large onions, chopped

1 bunch scallions, chopped

3 stalks celery, chopped

1 large green bell pepper, chopped

At least 3 cloves garlic, minced

Smoked pork sausage or andouille, amount depends on how much turkey you're using

Gravy from Thanksgiving turkey, including any vegetables in the gravy

Water, broth, or wine

Leftover turkey carcass, with the meat removed and reserved

Bay leaf or two

1 tablespoon grated lemon rind

½ teaspoon dried thyme

1 whole clove

Salt and pepper to taste

Bunch of parsley, chopped

For serving: leftover cornbread or bread dressing, filé, and hot sauce

1. In a large, heavy-bottomed Dutch oven, make a dark roux by constantly stirring the flour with the vegetable oil over medium heat. When the roux has reached the color of dark chocolate, add the chopped onions and scallions. Stir constantly and carefully until the onions to begin to caramelize, about 5 minutes.

2. Stir in the celery and bell pepper, and then garlic. When the vegetables are all soft, add the sausage. Stir the sausage until it's brown, about 5 minutes, then add the leftover gravy and any gravy vegetables. Add stock or water to cover everything in the pot, then add the turkey carcass.

3. Cut leftover turkey meat into bite-sized pieces. Add the turkey meat, the bay leaves, lemon rind, thyme, and clove. Simmer at least 2 hours, so the flavors can meld.

4. When ready to serve, taste and adjust the seasonings, especially the salt and pepper. Stir in the chopped parsley. Remove and discard the carcass. Serve the gumbo in bowls over leftover dressing with filé and hot sauce on the side.

CRANBERRY SAUCE

MAKES 2 CUPS

This recipe makes a delicious homemade, tart cranberry sauce that's not too sweet. Enjoy it alongside roasted turkey, roasted chicken, or ham. It also tastes great on cornbread, or if you make a turkey and dressing sandwich. But do not overlook the best possibility: if you make Turkey Bone Gumbo after a turkey feast from the recipe above, use cornbread and oyster dressing instead of rice in the bowl, then add a dollop of this sauce into the hot steaming bowl. It is unforgettable. (This recipe is also a good way to use the jars of pepper jelly sitting in your cupboard.)

1 pound fresh cranberries

1 (8-ounce) jar homemade pepper jelly or marmalade

1. In a microwaveable bowl add the cranberries and the jelly. Cover with a vented top and microwave on high 3 minutes.

2. Stir well, cover again, and microwave on high 4 minutes more. Serve cold or at room temperature.

SEAFOOD GUMBO

MAKES 8 SERVINGS

1. To make a roux, heat oil over medium heat in a large, heavy-bottomed pot. Add the flour and stir constantly until the mixture is the color between peanut butter and coffee grounds. Be careful not to burn it.

2. When the roux has reached the proper color, carefully add the onions and cook, stirring often, until soft, 5 minutes. Stir in the celery and bell pepper and cook, stirring often, another 5 minutes. Add the garlic, then the stock, and stir well to incorporate.

3. Add the turkey necks, tomatoes, okra, bay leaves, and Creole seasoning. Simmer an hour. Taste for salt and pepper and adjust seasoning. Add the shrimp and crabs. After broth comes back to a simmer, cook 10 more minutes. Remove the gumbo from the heat and stir in filé. Serve hot in a soup or gumbo bowl over rice.

½ cup vegetable oil, bacon fat, or duck fat

½ cup all-purpose flour

2 cups chopped onions

1 cup chopped celery

1 cup chopped bell pepper

3 cloves garlic, minced

1 gallon hot seafood stock

1 pound smoked turkey necks

1 pint fresh tomatoes, chopped

1 pound okra, sliced into coins

2 bay leaves

Creole seasoning to taste

Salt and pepper to taste

1 pound peeled shrimp

1 pound cleaned gumbo crabs

2 tablespoons filé

For serving: hot cooked rice

ZUPPA DI PESCE (FISH SOUP)

1. Place a large, heavy pot over medium heat and heat the olive oil. Sauté the onions until soft, about 5 minutes. Add the garlic, raisins, capers, and cardamom and cook an additional 3 minutes.

2. Stir in the parsley, tomato, wine, and stock and bring to a gentle simmer. Add the fish, shrimp, and clams and simmer 10 minutes. Taste for salt and pepper. Serve hot in bowls garnished with mint, olives, and orange zest.

¼ cup olive oil

1 medium onion, chopped

3 cloves garlic, minced

1 tablespoon golden raisins

1 tablespoon chopped capers

½ teaspoon ground cardamom

2 bunches parsley, chopped

1 tomato, chopped

2 cups white wine or vermouth

2 cups fish stock

2 pounds mixed fish filets, cut into pieces, and peeled shrimp or small clams

Salt and pepper to taste

For serving: 1 cup chopped mint, ½ cup chopped green olives, grated zest of one orange

LENTIL SOUP

MAKES 6 SERVINGS

This recipe gives you the chance to use any leftovers in the refrigerator. A piece of squash, a chunk of eggplant, a bit of fennel—all you have to do is chop it up and add it to the soup.

1. Heat the oil over medium heat in a large soup pot and add the onion, carrots, and celery. Cook until onion is golden, 10 to 15 minutes, stirring occasionally. Add the water, lentils, garlic, bay leaves, seasoning mix, and whatever additional vegetables you have found in the refrigerator. If you have none, that's fine. You just don't want this to be a missed opportunity to use them.

2. Simmer until lentils are tender, about 45 minutes. Add salt and pepper to taste. Dish out the soup and top each serving with about a teaspoon of olive oil and a shake of smoked paprika.

3 tablespoons vegetable oil or bacon fat

1 medium onion, chopped

2 carrots, chopped

2 stalks celery, chopped

2 quarts water

1 pound dried lentils

5 cloves garlic, minced

2 bay leaves

1 tablespoon Creole Italian Seasoning Mix (recipe page 23)

Salt and pepper to taste

For serving: good olive oil and smoked paprika

CHAPTER 5

TRADITIONS

Eggs and Bread

Remember, my sweet protector, St. Joseph, that no one ever had recourse to your protection or
implored your aid without obtaining relief. Confiding therefore in your goodness,
despise not my petitions . . . but graciously receive them. Amen.
—Part of prayer for blessing a St. Joseph altar

During my childhood I certainly didn't forget I was of Sicilian heritage. How could I? Every day I interacted with family members who had been born in Sicily, and I constantly heard their native language spoken. But my children did not know my grandparents, who had passed on before they were born. My children did not have firsthand experience with any Sicilian immigrants and therefore did not know what it meant to hold on to a language and food, even while becoming more and more American.

My mother, my children's Nana, tried to keep up traditions. But the old Sicilian community was quickly dwindling, and without their support these rituals were hard to maintain. And my children resisted. They failed to see the logic in "old-fashioned" tradition.

ST. JOSEPH ALTARS

One extremely important tradition is the preparation of food-laden altars every March 19 to honor Sicily's favorite saint, St. Joseph. My mother's name was Josephine, so St. Joseph was her personal patron saint.

When I was a child, we made many a pilgrimage around the city to visit altars. But to my kids, going around to St. Joseph altars and watching children pretend to be Mary and Joseph was just not exciting stuff. Neither was having an elderly aunt explain that if you were good, maybe one day you could be part of the ceremony. Couple that with cookies that, in their minds, reeked of anise, a flavor unappealing to most American children, and St. Joseph altars seemed appallingly out of sync with modern sensibilities.

Interestingly, over the years the St. Joseph altar tradition has changed to fit into modern life. One difference is that instead of hosting St. Joseph altars in home, churches are stepping up as main venues. This saves private hosts a tremendous amount of time, work, and inconvenience.

Another change is the way the enormous amount of food for altars is prepared. With so many women working outside the home, finding time to make thousands of cookies is a tedious and lonely task. Historically many took on this job with friends and members of their church. Then, instead of saying a prayer while baking each cookie, they'd have conversations while they worked. Today, a huge time saver is the abundance of ready-made St. Joseph cookies and breads available in local grocery stores and bakeries. In the months leading to March 19 it's no longer necessary to labor constantly in a kitchen; a day or two before, you can run out and build your altar from grocery shelves.

If you do bake your own, today it's perfectly acceptable to exchange anise oil for almond oil, or even vanilla, so that traditional cookies, which are not as sweet as what today's children expect, will be eaten and not ignored.

Would St. Joseph care? The past few decades have witnessed the secularization of St. Joseph altars. Breads are made in nontraditional shapes, and many of the foods are not of Sicilian origin. The Catholic archbishop of New Orleans embraces these changes, and he's probably like me, facing the realization that this tradition must either adapt to the times or die. The idea of creating a public altar for cultural reasons is fun and promises to spur the altars to spread, except, of course, to my own children, who are not even casually interested. The older of my two granddaughters, however, keeps asking me what a St. Joseph altar is for.

Without the religious underpinning, that is a difficult question to answer.

WOMEN ARE PEOPLE TOO!

Throughout my years growing up, I found it ironic that, despite the prejudice Sicilians had experienced collectively, the organized Italian community itself was extraordinarily sexist. It seemed crazy that all the organizations that celebrated Italian heritage were exclusively for men. Women could only belong to auxiliary organizations. The New Orleans Sicilian community was so male oriented that when I married in 1970, because of my lineage my totally non-Italian husband could join any Italian heritage organization in New Orleans. But I could only join the auxiliary.

It finally dawned on me that there was no end to the irrational Sicilian prejudice against women. I found the vestige of the Old World attitudes difficult to swallow. Rather than dealing with the stupidity, I chose to avoid that prejudice when possible, so I never joined any of the numerous local Italian heritage societies. Today, things have improved. In particular, if anyone is of Italian heritage or even interested in Italian culture, they're qualified to belong to most Italian heritage organizations.

I understand where the sexist attitudes of the Italian heritage organizations came from, as I saw it firsthand in my family. My mother and I were a disappointment to my Papa because we were not male. My mother was an only child, so his desire for a male heir was never realized. As a result, my poor mother was practically rendered schizophrenic by the simultaneous desire to be what my grandfather really wanted her to be, that is, a boy, and what he said he wanted, which was for her to be a proper young lady who was modest, retiring, beautiful, and virtuous. I found Papa's way of

Mother and me

thinking terribly insensitive, and perhaps that is what made the whole community's narrow-minded attitude so intolerable.

I suppose I picked up part of my way of thinking from my mother. Her whole life she was tortured by "what-ifs," and she did not want me to grow up with similar regrets. So she lived her life through me, and she always encouraged me to do whatever I wanted. No holding back, despite the family's views. The carte blanche she gave me was first challenged when, in the ever-changing environment when I was trying on different roles, I told her I wanted to be a doctor. My Papa said no, a nurse. My mother told him I could be a doctor if I wanted, and she insisted that he not relay his objections to me. Ever slippery. So Papa agreed I

could be a pediatrician, but not a surgeon. My mother was furious. Another time I said I wanted to be a pilot so that I could become an astronaut, and he told me I had to be a stewardess. Again, my mother set him straight.

Surprisingly, his views had somewhat changed by the time I said I wanted to be a teacher. He counseled that I should tell my mother I wanted to be a principal (at least) or a college professor. (For the record, I ended up going to law school.) Regardless, he was always thrilled that my mother had married my father, the American, who did not find my mother's more feminist ways a problem. Deep inside, I'm sure Papa knew that women would one day acquire the respectability his only daughter craved, and he knew that while she was fighting for it, she was in good hands.

My mother had grown up at the time when women won the right the vote, began wearing bloomers, and stopped riding side-saddle. She married respectably, then she had my grandfather's first grandchild, me, a girl. Finally, after five years, my brother followed, redeeming my mother in Papa's eyes. But I was so much older than my brother, Colin, that by the time of his birth, my Papa had already brought me into the financial world, in case there never would be a grandson.

During the time Papa was seemingly resigned to not having a grandson, he would take me to the overwhelmingly male-dominated offices of Merrill Lynch. Wearing a nice dress and gloves, I would sit with him in a fancy room, watching the numbers on the big stock boards change. He would assign me several stocks to watch. He would watch a few others, the whole while taking notes on the envelope notepads my Nana made. Afterward, we'd walk to a restaurant and eat club sandwiches cut into triangles, with the crusts removed. There was always a toothpick with a cellophane flourish on top. At some restaurants the toothpick was a little sword. Those were my favorite.

ALL IN THE NAME

As I see it now, I have become totally American. Although I am named for my grandmother, Elisabetta, I am called Elizabeth, a move that has my grandfather's fingerprints all over it. He, of course, had legally abandoned being Francesco to become Frank. I am now mostly known as Liz, and my father's last name was Williams. As Liz Williams, my name gives no clue to my being half Sicilian.

Everything I learned growing up was Italian, or maybe Sicilian, which was really a culture frozen in time starting from the day my grandmother and her parents set foot in New Orleans. This resistance to change afflicted New Orleans's tens of thousands of Sicilian immigrants. Italy certainly had been changing, and my grandparents unknowingly continued to change, but Italy and my grandparents did not change in a parallel way. So what I thought of as Italian culture and beliefs was a retelling of someone else's memories. And those memories were from another generation and another time.

That is true about the food memories too. A trip to Sicily revealed that the food there is nothing but a touchstone of the Creole Italian food we eat in New Orleans. The roots are visible, but the leaves and flowers are different. We only fool ourselves into thinking that what we eat here is Italian.

My mother once took a trip to Sicily with her cousin, who was also named Josephine. (They were known to our family as Jo and Fini—Jo was my mother, and Fini my mother's cousin.) While in Palermo, my mother asked the Sicilian guide to help her find her family on her mother's side, that is, my Nana's

side. She told the guide the family name was Lecce. The guide tried to narrow the search field, so she asked my mother whether she was from the Jewish Lecce family or the group that had converted to Catholicism. This was the first time we learned we might have Jewish ancestry.

With a modicum of research I learned there was a large Jewish ghetto in the town of Lecce, in Italy's southeastern heel. There, Jews had at one time been a thriving part of the city, involved with the markets and the economy in general. However, during the reign of King Ferdinand I and the environment of intolerance he created, the Jews were massacred. The Jewish ghetto in the town was torched until it burned to the ground, basically obliterating any evidence of Jewish life in Lecce.

Those who survived and escaped moved to other places, including Sicily. It was a common practice to take the name of the place from which you came, so Jews settling in Palermo from Lecce became So-and-So di Lecce, which finally became merely Lecce. There were enough Jews from Lecce that the surname became an indicator of being Jewish. There also must have been a concern for safety, because some Jews converted to Catholicism. History tells us that many Jews became Christians to escape persecution or, more desperately, to escape being killed.

Forced conversion adds another layer of complexity and sadness to the story of the Lecces. And after a great number of generations spanning hundreds of years, the connections of my family to the town of Lecce and of being Jewish have been lost. It seems we descended from a group of Lecces who had converted to the dominant and favored religion of Italy, Roman Catholicism, which was the religion of my family when they arrived in the United States. The shocking part is that my mother did not know anything about our

Jewish roots. By the time she first went to Sicily, my Nana had already died, so there was no asking her. She asked my great-uncle, who grew up in the same house with my mother and was only two years her senior, but he did not know anything about our Jewish relations or Jewish heritage either.

The loss of records makes tracing individual Lecces impossible. But I do know that some Jews who lived in Palermo became butchers. Although I am sure he was a Catholic, my great-grandfather was also a butcher, working in the French Market of New Orleans. Was that a confluence of coincidences or a trade handed down through the generations? And what about butchers, frugal as they are, who are known to eat offal? A famous sandwich in Palermo is *pani cà meusa,* a very greasy spleen sandwich that is definitely an acquired taste. Even with all the butchers from Palermo in my family, a spleen sandwich was only a legend and not something we regularly ate. I have not explored our Jewish roots, but it is something I plan to do in the future.

DEVELOPING TASTES

Sicilians tend to coddle their children, and my mother was no exception, especially when it came to food. As a child I loved brussels sprouts. When my mother went to the grocery store, I would sit in the seat of the cart demanding that she buy them. And she would. Never following a recipe, she'd chop them and sauté them with bacon or butter and caramelize them, sometimes with balsamic vinegar. I loved the slightly bitter flavor. My mother served wonderful brussels sprouts.

I think my mother enjoyed the novelty of a child who liked brussels sprouts, and I think I inherited a love for bitter. I crave slaw made with radicchio, pasta with broccoli rabe, and dark chocolate. My grand-mother's candied citrus peel was a favorite candy, and she candied grapefruit peel just for me. The bittersweet flavor of the candied grapefruit peel is the metaphor of life. My love of bitter was indulged by my family, and I exploited it.

There is certainly a plethora of Italian flavors that capitalize on bitter. Liqueurs made from artichoke, apéritifs such as Campari, and desserts made with bitter almonds all evoke the bitter flavor. But being in America made my enjoyment of the bitter unusual.

My mother, facing a child who wasn't asking for candy, was indulgent. She served leftover bitter vegetables cold or at room temperature with *agliata.* Cold cooked greens—straight from the refrigerator—were delicious on a bacon sandwich, or tossed with just-cooked pasta for a quick meatless meal. My father, who loved collard greens, mustard greens, and turnip greens, was happy to let Mother wash mustard greens three times for me. Then he would raise a fork to me in thanks, because he would enjoy the greens, too. He would also often suggest to me that we hadn't had mustard greens in a long time, and I would immediately ask for them.

THE 1960S: A TYPICAL AMERICAN FAMILY

When I was young, my grandfather still worked alongside my father in our family's freight-forwarding agency. My mother eventually worked at their office, but while I was young, our home and my grandparents' home were female enclaves during the day (until my brother was born).

After work, my father would take a downtown bus to our Lakeview home on Canal Boulevard. Our street was divided by a large neutral ground (boulevard). A bus stop was directly across the street, and on weekdays a little before 6:00 p.m. I would play in the front yard and wait for the buses that regularly passed on the other side of the boulevard. That was the direction of the buses coming from downtown, in the Central Business District. When one stopped at the corner I would look for my father. When he crossed the street and stepped onto our block, I would run to meet him. When we met, he'd lean down, scoop me into his arms, swing me around, and carry me into the house.

My father would hang up his jacket and take off his tie, and we would sit down to dinner. My mother wore aprons, and she would set the table over an oil-cloth cover. Once he was old enough, my little brother would sit in his high chair, wearing a bib. By then I was old enough to empty the ice trays into a bowl and fill the glasses with ice. We drank unsweetened iced tea every night. This was typical New Orleans, but I didn't know it.

At that table I would put my napkin on my lap. Dinner conversation revolved around what we'd done that day. What was on our plates came from my mother's repertoire: pastas and other Sicilian foods, New Orleans cuisine with my mother's personal twist, and food typical of the fifties. For a special treat we had pie or cake. When my father was out of town on business, my mother served the most special treat for me, frozen TV dinners. They really didn't taste good, but it was a thrill to eat from a little aluminum tray with compartments on a TV table and actually watching TV.

CREOLE SICILIAN SHAKSHUKA (EGGS POACHED IN TOMATO SAUCE)

MAKES 2 SERVINGS

This recipe could reflect the period when Arabs ruled Sicily around the ninth century, when so many Catholic churches were converted to mosques. On second thought, this dish seems extremely Mediterranean, and since Sicily is right there in the Mediterranean, a Sicilian version of this dish would not be a surprise.

When there was only a bit left of Nana's ever-simmering pot of tomato sauce, she would make baked eggs. This is her shakshuka, a dish called by many different names throughout the Mediterranean. Her recipe calls for cooking down chopped onion and garlic and throwing in leftover artichokes, broccoli, shrimp, or crab. When everything was hot, she would add a few ladlesful of tomato sauce and crack in the eggs. If the oven was on for another dish, she'd pop the pan in the oven. If not, she'd put a cover on the pan and cook it on top of the stove.

This dish is another example of how technique and methodology, as opposed to a firm and unyielding recipe, are the legacy of the Sicilian immigrants. I learned to take what was there, in the refrigerator or in the pantry, and make it into something delicious. Do not waste is the Sicilian prime directive.

2 tablespoons olive oil

½ medium onion, chopped

1 cup sliced bell peppers, mixed colors, or other leftover vegetables

2 cloves garlic, minced

2 cups Nana's Basic Tomato Sauce, heated through (recipe page 20)

4 large eggs

For serving: ½ cup chopped herbs, grated Parmesan cheese, and hot sauce

1. Heat your oven to 375°F. Over medium-high heat, heat the olive oil in an ovenproof skillet. Sauté the onion, bell peppers, and garlic until soft. Add hot tomato sauce.

2. Carefully break the eggs into the tomato sauce and place the uncovered skillet in the hot oven 20 to 25 minutes, depending on how you like your eggs. If desired, sprinkle with chopped herbs and cheese, and spice it up with hot sauce.

DEVILED EGGS

MAKES 12 DEVILED EGGS

My Nana had not encountered deviled eggs until she came to America. She judged them a great snack, but sort of bland, so she set to work doctoring them up with her own familiar flavors. Basil was a favorite enhancer, but when there was none available fresh she would sometimes mash a piece of anchovy into mayonnaise and tapenade and mix that with the egg yolk stuffing.

Unlike most southerners, Nana did not have a special deviled egg serving plate. (I have several, being a modern southern woman.) To keep the slippery eggs from sliding all over, she'd line a plate or platter with a thick layer of dried beans and nestle in the stuffed eggs, which tidily stayed put.

6 large hard-boiled eggs, peeled

¼ cup mayonnaise

1 tablespoon Dijon mustard

2 teaspoons good extra-virgin olive oil

¼ teaspoon salt

¼ teaspoon pepper

1 teaspoon smoked paprika

6 black olives, cut in half

Optional garnishes: curls of Parmesan cheese or other hard Italian cheese, a mound of tapenade, or pieces of crisp bacon

1. Halve the eggs lengthwise. Gently remove the yolks and put them into a 1-quart bowl. To the yolks add the mayonnaise, mustard, olive oil, salt, and pepper. With a fork or the back of a spoon, mash the ingredients together until they form a smooth paste. Taste a tiny amount and adjust the salt and pepper.

2. Place the paste into a self-closing plastic sandwich bag and squeeze the paste into one corner. Cut off the tip of the bag corner and evenly squeeze and distribute the paste among the egg whites. Place the paprika into a small strainer and lightly dust the filled eggs. Stand an olive half in each yolk, and garnish with optional cheese, tapenade, or bacon. Cover and refrigerate until ready to serve.

PANI CÀ MEUSA
(PANE CON LA MILZA—BEEF SPLEEN SANDWICHES)

MAKES AS MANY AS YOU WANT

1. Soak the spleen strips in the milk and place in the refrigerator overnight.

2. When ready to cook, cut the rolls in half horizontally. Discard the soaking milk and dry the spleen strips with paper towels. In a large skillet set over medium-high heat, heat the beef fat until it bubbles. Carefully add the spleen and stir and cook until the strips are crispy and change color to a sort of dark gray.

3. Place a generous pile of hot spleen on the bottom of each sandwich roll. Sprinkle with salt and pepper, top with ¼ cup of cheese, and then with the remaining roll halves. Serve with a lemon quarter.

Beef spleen, sliced into strips

Milk

Round sandwich rolls

Rendered beef fat

Salt and pepper

¼ cup caciocavallo cheese per sandwich

For serving: lemon quarters

ITALIAN SWEETBREAD SANDWICHES

MAKES 4 SERVINGS

If you cannot get spleen or you just find it unappealing, I suggest this cheating version using sweetbreads.

1. Soak the sweetbreads in the milk 4 hours in the refrigerator. Discard the milk and pat the sweetbreads dry.

2. When ready to cook, slice the rolls in half horizontally. If you want, you can toast them. Heat the butter in a small sauté pan over a medium flame. Cook the sweetbreads in the hot pan on both sides until done, about 3 minutes per side. Squeeze the juice of the lemon quarter onto the sweetbreads.

3. Place the hot sweetbreads on the bottoms of the split roll. Sprinkle with salt and pepper. Place ¼ cup cheese over the warm sweetbreads in each sandwich. Top with the remaining roll halves and serve.

4 sweetbreads, trimmed

Milk

4 round sandwich rolls

2 or 3 tablespoons butter

¼ lemon

Salt and pepper

1 cup caciocavallo cheese (or ricotta salata)

CREOLE CREAM CHEESE AND FIGS

MAKES 3 OR 4 CUPS

While trying to figure out which chapter should include this recipe, I decided that the one on bread was the right place. This iconic Creole breakfast dish just has to be eaten on really crusty braided Italian bread.

Fig trees used to be extremely common in New Orleans, and on many hot July mornings I'd be sent out to our yard to collect fresh figs from our tree.

Creole cream cheese is a tart, fresh cheese, and its flavor depends on the yeasts floating in the air. Up until the 1970s, Creole cream cheese, made both commercially and in homes, was extremely popular on New Orleans breakfast tables. Today, it's more likely to appear in ice cream, producing a slightly tart ice cream that is much more flavorful than those made with yogurt. Me, I still like it spread on bread with fresh fruit or preserves. And if I've eaten too much for lunch, it makes a wonderful light supper.

1 gallon skim milk, unhomogenized, if possible (definitely not super-pasteurized or irradiated)

1 cup buttermilk

6 to 8 drops rennet

Cheesecloth

For serving: half-and-half, fresh figs, and braided Italian bread

1. In a large glass or stainless-steel bowl, combine the skim milk, the buttermilk, and the rennet. (Start with 6 drops rennet. If your milk comes from a dairy that uses ultrahigh processing temperatures, which changes the milk's proteins, you might have to use up to 8 drops.) Cover with plastic wrap and allow to sit at room temperature until the mixture clabbers, when the whey rises to the top and the curds sink to the bottom. This will take at least 24 hours, but could take up to 36.

2. Line a large colander with 2 or 3 layers of dampened cheesecloth, depending on the tightness of the weave. Drain the clabbered curds through the cheesecloth placed in the colander. (If you want, save the drained whey, which is wonderful in making cornbread or yeast bread.) After you have removed as much liquid as possible, cover the top of the colander with plastic wrap, place it in a large bowl, and place the bowl in the refrigerator. Allow the cheese to drain 48 hours.

3. By now, the cheese should be firm yet soft. Serve it in a bowl topped with half-and-half and fresh figs, and smear some on slices of Italian bread.

SEASONED BREADCRUMBS

MAKES 3–5 CUPS, DEPENDING ON THE TYPE OF
BREAD YOU USE AND HOW DRY IT IS

A review of stuffed vegetable recipes in southern cookbooks reveals that in the American South rice is the starch of choice for fillings. Even mainstream Stouffer's uses rice as the starch in its frozen stuffed peppers. But in New Orleans, we stuff vegetables the frugal Sicilian way, with seasoned breadcrumbs. We probably can't prove that New Orleans cooks adopted this practice from the Sicilians. But regardless, we eat it that way.

Coming from Sicily, a place where people were constantly hungry, even stale bread was too precious to discard. Aside from its use as stuffing for vegetables, breadcrumbs formed an important base for thickening soups and sauces, for topping vegetables, and for extending salads. Today, seasoned breadcrumbs in New Orleans means Italian seasoning with dried oregano, and often Parmesan cheese. And there's no denying the Sicilian roots of putting Parmesan cheese in stuffed crabs made with breadcrumbs, even though it defies the Italian edict not to mix cheese and seafood.

This recipe can be the base of any stuffed vegetable, which can be enhanced with seafood, sausage, or chopped ham, as well as the trinity of onion, bell pepper, and celery, or any other seasoning vegetable. You can also use these crumbs in meatballs, as breading for paneed meat, and to thicken soups.

8 ounces stale bread

¼ cup olive oil

1 tablespoon dried oregano

1 tablespoon dried parsley

1 tablespoon dried basil

Dried red peppers to taste

¼ cup freshly grated Parmesan cheese

1. Preheat your oven to 200°F. Grate the bread into crumbs or whirl it in a food processor until all of the bread is crumbed. Place the oil in a rimmed sheet pan or cookie sheet and completely coat the bottom.

2. In a large bowl, evenly mix together the breadcrumbs, oregano, parsley, dried basil, and red peppers. Spread the mixture onto the cookie sheet in an even layer. Bake 5 minutes. Remove the pan, stir well, and spread the mixture back into an even layer. Return to the oven 5 more minutes.

3. Allow the mixture to cool. Add the cheese and mix well. Store in an airtight container at room temperature.

AGLIATA (BREAD AND GARLIC SAUCE)

MAKES 1½ CUPS

Agliata was another way to use up leftover bread. This creamy condiment is sort of like Italian mayonnaise, and it's great on boiled and grilled meat, fish, and vegetables, or on just about anything that could benefit from a sauce. To Nana, oil and eggs were considered expensive, so using something like this wonderful, fresh-tasting spread could substitute for mayonnaise in many cold dishes. I used to like it on sandwiches. *Agliata* was my secret ingredient to making the best southern tomato sandwich, BLT, and po'boy you could eat. Duke's and Blue Plate—eat your hearts out.

2 cups stale bread, without crusts and cut in cubes

Water

3 tablespoons red wine vinegar

2 cloves garlic

½ cup olive oil

3 tablespoons fresh flat-leaf parsley leaves

3 tablespoons of another fresh green herb, such as mint, basil, or tarragon, depending on the dish accompanying the *Agliata*

Salt to taste

1. Place the bread in a bowl and cover it with enough water to thoroughly wet all the bread cubes. When the bread has absorbed all the water, squeeze it as dry as possible with your hands. Discard the liquid and place the squeezed bread into the bowl of a food processor.

2. Add the vinegar and garlic and process. When the mixture reaches the consistency of paste, add the olive oil in a drizzle with the processor running. When the mixture turns fluffy, add the herbs and salt and pulse to incorporate, without making the herbs disappear. Store covered in the refrigerator up to a week.

CORNBREAD

MAKES AN 8- OR 9-INCH CORNBREAD

My father was very much a Louisianan, and he loved cornbread, not too sweet. He'd use it to sop up potlikker, and he especially enjoyed it with the juice from turnip greens with pickled pork.

Because of my Sicilian mother, he was inundated with braised vegetables other than the familiar mustard and turnip greens from his childhood. But he never gave up the southern habit of using cornbread to soak up potlikker from any kind of bitter greens, including the very Italian broccoli rabe. So my mother increasingly served cornbread with her more Italian-inspired meals, and my father adapted by using it to soak up the garlicky olive oil and lemon liquid leftover from the broccoli, zucchini, or whatever vegetables my mother might have cooked.

If you use cornbread to soak up juice from salty vegetables, you'll be glad it isn't too sweet. If you're not into soaking up potlikker, you can eat cornbread a few other ways my father liked, with butter or dipped in the grease from just-cooked sausage.

¼ cup bacon fat

1 cup yellow cornmeal

1 cup all-purpose flour

2 tablespoons sugar

4 teaspoons baking powder

½ teaspoon salt

1 cup water

1 large egg, beaten

1. Preheat your oven to 400°F. Place the bacon fat into an 8- or 9-inch cast-iron skillet. Place the skillet into the hot oven at least 10 minutes. In the meantime, in a bowl whisk together the cornmeal, flour, sugar, baking powder, and salt. Add the water and egg to the dry ingredients and mix until everything is absorbed.

2. Take the skillet from the oven and swirl the fat around to grease the insides. Pour the excess fat into the cornbread batter and mix well. Use a paper towel to carefully rub the grease remaining in the pan into the entire inside surface.

3. Add the batter to the hot skillet and shake from side to side to level it. (If necessary, use an offset spatula to spread the batter.) Reduce the baking temperature to 350°F and place the skillet into the oven. Bake until the cornbread begins to come away from the sides, about 45 minutes. Let cool 5 minutes, then cut into wedges. Serve warm with a pie server.

SFINCIONE (SICILIAN PIZZA)

MAKES 2 LARGE PIZZAS

This traditional flatbread, often served on New Year's Eve, is not as thin-crusted as the pizza we know here in America. This is definitely an embellished flatbread, with some chew to it. It is eaten with a fork and knife hot from the oven. Cold, it can be taken to work for lunch and eaten with your hands.

In addition to the toppings in the ingredient list, you might also add sliced red bell peppers, Italian sausage, black olives, or mushrooms. Just use your imagination. For authenticity, however, Sicilian pizza usually does not have mozzarella cheese; it uses caciocavallo, the same cheese used traditionally in the spleen sandwich *pani cà meusa*. This semi-hard cheese has a smooth yellow rind and is popular all over Sicily. It's usually made of sheep's milk and allowed to hang, which gives the cheese a teardrop shape. If you cannot get caciocavallo, you can generally substitute provolone, or use any cheese you like.

Sometimes my Nana would top her *sfincione* with sliced fresh tomatoes. But usually she used homemade tomato sauce, the kind made with canned tomatoes.

My Papa was a big fan of *sfincione*. For some reason, my Nana usually made it when he worked in the yard. I remember one day I was given the job of sweeping the leaves off the sidewalk that led to my grandparents' front door. In the middle of the job, my Nana called us in for lunch, and as I went in I stood the broom against the wall on the front porch. When returning to our yard work, my grandfather walked out the front door with me, saw my broom, and grew extremely disturbed. Although he rarely spoke of the mafia, feeling it made him less American to be aware of this group of organized criminals, he certainly was aware, or seemed to be aware of it. In this case he instructed me that leaving a broom on your front porch was a sign of sympathy with the mafia, and that I should never leave a broom on the front porch for any reason. So I never did it again.

PIZZA DOUGH

1½ cups warm water (about 100°F)

2 packages dry yeast

½ teaspoon salt

4 cups all-purpose flour (or half all-purpose and half semolina, or your favorite proportions), divided

½ cup olive oil, approximately

TOPPINGS

Tomato sauce

Anchovies

Onions

Oregano

Breadcrumbs

Cooked sausage

Olives

Caciocavallo cheese

1. In a large bowl, add the water then stir in the yeast. In a separate bowl, mix the salt into 3 cups of the flour. Stir the salted flour into the water and yeast.

2. Sprinkle about ½ cup of the remaining flour onto a hard surface. Flour your hands, place the dough onto the surface, and knead until the dough is smooth, about 5 minutes. Place the dough into an oiled bowl, cover with a towel, and let it rise in a warm place until doubled in bulk, about 30 minutes.

3. After the dough has doubled, place a pizza stone in your oven and heat it to 425°F. Oil 2 jelly roll pans. Divide the dough in 2 and stretch each half into rectangles, or any shape you want that will fit on the prepared pans. Lay the stretched dough halves onto the pans and cover them lightly with sauce. Layer on the toppings and sprinkle with grated caciocavallo cheese. Slide the pizzas directly onto the hot stone and bake until brown and bubbly, about 15 minutes. Cut into squares and serve.

CHAPTER 6

THE VERY BEGINNING
Seafood

Whatever may happen to the Sicilians, they comment on it with a joke.
—Cicero, Roman orator

There have been Italians in New Orleans since before the French christened the city as la Nouvelle Orléans. René-Robert Cavelier, Sieur de la Salle, French explorer of the mouth of the Mississippi River in the 1680s, was accompanied by Enrico de Tonti, a Neapolitan turned French soldier. (French records list him as Henri.) La Salle left Tonti in the region to work on the French claim to the area. Tonti is memorialized in the name of a city street.

In the 1540s, even before the time of La Salle, Hernando de Soto had included Italians in his exploration party. Many Europeans were choosing to explore and settle in this new and exciting world for a variety of reasons, and people from city-states throughout the Italian peninsula were among them. Like most, they

were eager to find new opportunities, and they came from all over Italy to make their fortunes.

When the city of New Orleans was formally established in 1718, Italians were among the many who arrived that year on the ship *Chameau*. This group came from the northern regions of Italy, such as Piedmont and Liguria. These early immigrants and their descendants became part of the city's original establishment, participating in such as diverse ways as serving on the *cabildo,* the city council, or as *alcalde ordinario,* a city official.

Giuseppe Maria Francesco Vigo of Mondovi served in the Spanish army in New Orleans in the 1770s, and he later supported the Americans in the Revolutionary War. Most of the Italians who came to New Orleans during this period were affiliated with the military. They intermarried with locals and settled into the life in the Creole city. However, another group of Italians who came during this early period were those who had immigrated to France and were brought here by the French as part of the groups of vagabonds who originally settled the new city.

By the early nineteenth century, the city of New Orleans was part of the United States. It had an important place on the Mississippi River, and its growing American commercial and cultural identity made it an important city of consulates and trade offices. New Orleans received goods from around the world, and it also collected and sent American products to the rest of the world. It was an international city where people from different cultures could feel comfortable.

EARLY TASTES OF ACHIEVEMENT

Local consular offices included those from many of the various Italian states, and many Italians became established in New Orleans and the surrounding areas. The Italians who came before the mass Sicilian migration were often artisans, such as masons or architects, or artists who contributed to cultural life. These Italians became involved with city life, but they did not seem to have a deep impact on the city's food. They also did not reach a critical mass that created an enclave of Italians, so they became assimilated into the city without publicly retaining their Italian identity.

Pierre Maspero was a Milanese who first operated a New Orleans slave exchange and later opened a coffeehouse known as Maspero's Exchange. In the WPA guidebook to New Orleans, it is called the Exchange Coffee House. In the spirit of early restaurants, Maspero's was a meeting place as well as an eatery, and it is believed that Andrew Jackson and his followers met

there to make plans for the Battle of New Orleans. Some members of the pirate Jean Lafitte's band of smugglers were Italians, and they participated in that battle. A look at some of the city's businesses with Italian names shows the strong pull of food culture: Maspero with a coffee shop, Socola with his rice production, and Oteri with his fruit importation.

Angelo Socola, from the northwestern Italian city of San Remo, was notable in the New Orleans food industry. For a short time he was part of an import company that brought in products from Mexico and Italy. Using steam-powered threshing machines, in the mid-nineteenth century he established what was considered the largest rice mill in the United States. He also planted different varieties of rice, and he is widely considered Louisiana's "Father of the Rice Industry."

In the mid-1800s, Santo Oteri created a company that became part of the United Fruit Company. Oteri purchased and imported bananas from Central America, primarily Honduras, into the Port of New Orleans. The Vaccaro brothers, Joseph, Luca, and Felix, and the D'Antoni brothers formed the precursor to the also successful Standard Fruit Company.

The report of the census of 1850 notes that the 924 people from Italy in Louisiana represented the largest number of Italian immigrants in any U.S. state. During this period, Italian immigrants and their descendants participated in the Civil War in the Garibaldi Legion and in the Italian Guard Battalion. Francesco Maria de Reggio was the great-grandfather of Confederate general P. G. T. Beauregard.

MAKING IT ANY WAY THEY CAN

When the Italian states were finally unified between 1815 and 1879 in the movement known as Risorgimento, the nature of the opportunities for work in the southern part of Italy, especially for those on the island of Sicily, began to disappear. These events coincided with the end of the American Civil War. After the Civil War the Louisiana Bureau of Immigration recruited laborers from Sicily to replace the enslaved African Americans who had been emancipated. The Sicilian laborers who came during this period were de facto indentured servants and on their own, and they worked during the *zuccherrata* (sugarcane season).

The Immigration Bureau had offices in southern Italy, including Palermo, and arranged for labor transportation to Louisiana. Between 1880 and 1910, the State of Louisiana maintained these recruitment activities, bringing hundreds of Italian men to the state, where they lived in abandoned slave cabins. These Italian laborers paid rent for their accommodations, which was withheld from their wages, and often extended the agreed-upon time commitment necessary to pay back the costs of passage. Although the Sicilian recruits labored mainly in the cane fields, they also worked picking cotton and strawberries. Because Sicilian and African American laborers worked in the fields together engaging in the same backbreaking work, there were many opportunities for social and cultural exchange.

By the early 1900s about eighteen thousand primarily Sicilian workers were laboring in agriculture in Louisiana. At the time, the sugarcane industry was being undercut by cheaper labor in other countries, particularly in the Philippines. Local industry eventually employed fewer workers, forcing Sicilian field laborers to work in other industries. When they could leave the fields with a small monetary stake, many established farming operations in the parishes outside of New Orleans, as well as moving to New Orleans.

The huge bump of Sicilians who came to New Orleans after the Civil War and after the unification of Italy

paralleled the wave of Italian immigration through New York. There was already a base of Sicilians in New Orleans, so the geographic spread of Italians was not as broad here as it was at Ellis Island. That made the group of immigrants here more cohesive, especially since immigrants from all over Italy were still grappling with the concept of being Italian.

The thousands of immigrants and their solidarity had many effects on the Creole population in their new home. Some, such as the influence Sicilian immigration had on Creole food, were extremely positive. On the other hand, fear, caused by huge numbers of Sicilians, with their strange names, heavy accents, and different customs, also made many established citizens of New Orleans unwelcoming and hateful. This distrust, in turn, left many conventional doors to opportunity closed.

FOOD: A COMMON DENOMINATOR

Tracing census data from 1850, the massive number of Sicilians who eventually landed in the Port of New Orleans made the city at one time the largest Italian city in the United States. According to *Italians in New Orleans,* by Joseph Maselli and Dominic Candeloro, between 1898 and 1929 almost one hundred thousand Sicilians entered New Orleans. That's when my great-grandparents, Giuseppe Lecce and Francesca Paola Gambino Lecce, came with my then-eighteen-year-old grandmother, Elisabetta Lecce, along with several of her siblings. My grandmother had finished her high school education in Palermo and, like so many, arrived in New Orleans speaking no English. Although my great-grandfather died before I was born, he loomed large in myth. I do not have a photo of him, but I can imagine him as a butcher, wearing a dirty apron and wielding the huge knives my brother and I have inherited and treasure.

I did know my great-grandmother in the limited way many young children know their elder relatives. Reportedly a fantastic cook, she died before I was five years old, but I do remember visiting her and her speaking to me in the Sicilian dialect. Today, when I hear Sicilian spoken I do not understand it, but it does sound comforting.

The immigrants who came to New Orleans had no doubt suffered from the same sense of deprivation in their homeland as did the Italians who immigrated throughout the United States. And Italians generally, whether in New Orleans or elsewhere, were focused on the access to foods eaten by the wealthy but out of reach for them in Italy. In America, although most Italian immigrants faced discrimination, they also found abundance. And despite the early twentieth-century nutritionist movement that steered the population away from foods typical in the Italian diet, Italians all over America still influenced the way America ate.

I think it was easier for Sicilians to affect the food of New Orleans than it was to influence the rest of the country, mainly, as I've mentioned, because the general population in New Orleans was open to exploring new things, including unfamiliar food. Since New Orleans's food-snobbish Creoles understood that the Sicilians had a strong food culture too, they also understood that one's food culture is central to one's identity. And it is a happy fact that New Orleanians did not try to change the Sicilian way of eating. On the contrary, while the rest of the country was experimenting with nutrition and diet, the Creoles of New Orleans were exploring Sicilian food. And while the new national "healthy" way of eating slowed down Sicilian culinary assimilation in much of the United States, spaghetti and spumoni became common more quickly in New Orleans, the city with a curious palate.

FIG AND CRAB SALAD

MAKES 4 SERVINGS

A fig tree in your backyard is a blessing, but birds and squirrels become your enemy. When the figs ripen all at once you must think about all the things you can do with them, and think fast. This salad calls for fresh figs and reminds you that savory can be enhanced by sweet. I have sprinkled on all sorts of toppings, including blue cheese crumbles and Parmesan shavings. Once I turned this salad into a fancy lunch with a topping of lump crabmeat.

Place the figs, avocado, fennel, capers, and nuts into a large salad bowl. Drizzle on the olive oil and vinegar. Sprinkle with salt and pepper and toss well. Top with reserved fennel fronds. You can gild the lily with bacon crumbles or crabmeat.

6 fresh figs, cut into quarters

1 avocado, cut into rough chunks

1 fennel bulb, sliced thinly on a mandoline, fronds reserved

6 large capers, cut into quarters

½ cup roughly cut pecans, pistachios, almonds, or pine nuts (whatever you have, or a combination)

3 tablespoons good olive oil

1 tablespoon balsamic vinegar

Salt and pepper to taste

For serving: lump crabmeat and (optional) bacon crumbles

STUFFED CRABS

MAKES 4 STUFFED CRABS

1. Preheat oven to 325°F. Thoroughly wash the empty crab shells, or oil the glass crab shells, and set aside.

2. Add the olive oil to a sauté pan set over medium heat. When the oil is hot, add the onions and sauté until they are caramelized slightly, about 5 minutes. Add the celery and cook another 5 minutes. Add the claw meat, breaking it up as you cook it. When the crab is well mixed, place the mixture, including the oil, into a large bowl to cool about 5 minutes. (Because your hands are the best tools for the mixing and stuffing, the mixture needs to cool for your comfort.)

3. Add the breadcrumbs to the cooled crab mixture in the bowl and mix well. If it's too dry and does not stick together, add a bit of water or a bit more olive oil.

4. Divide the stuffing evenly among the 4 prepared shells, spooning it in compactly and mounding if necessary. Sprinkle the tops with the grated cheese. Place the crabs onto a sheet pan and bake 45 minutes. Serve warm.

4 empty crab shells or 4 glass crab shells

3 tablespoons olive oil

½ cup chopped onions

¼ cup chopped celery

1 pint crab claw meat

2 cups Seasoned Breadcrumbs (recipe page 101 or purchased)

¼ cup grated Parmesan cheese

SHRIMP AND FENNEL SALAD

MAKES 6 STARTER SERVINGS, OR 4 AS A MAIN MEAL

Good as a first course or light lunch.

1. Soak the onion slices in iced bowl of water. Meanwhile, in a large serving bowl, add the shrimp, fennel bulb slices, orange, and olives to a large serving bowl. Pour oil and lemon juice onto the contents in the bowl. Add salt and pepper and toss gently but thoroughly.

2. Drain the onion in a sieve and dry it with paper towels. Add the onion, avocado, and basil leaves to the bowl and gently toss again. Garnish with the fennel fronds. Serve immediately.

½ purple onion, sliced thinly on a mandoline

Bowl of water with 2 ice cubes

2 pounds cooked, peeled shrimp

1 fennel bulb, sliced thinly on a mandoline, fronds reserved

1 navel orange, sliced into supremes (segments), or a thinly sliced mango

1 cup pitted black olives, coarsely chopped

½ cup good extra-virgin olive oil

Juice of one lemon

Salt and pepper to taste

1 sliced avocado

5 large basil leaves, sliced in a chiffonade

GAMBERI CON ASPARAGI (SHRIMP WITH ASPARAGUS)

MAKES 4 SERVINGS

1. Fill a large skillet with water 1 inch from the top and bring to a simmer. Add the shrimp and asparagus, being careful not to break the delicate asparagus tips. Cook until the shrimp turn pink, about 4 minutes. Remove from the heat and carefully drain.

2. Toss the drained asparagus and shrimp into the buttered pasta along with the lemon rind and parsley. Divide among 4 bowls and serve immediately.

Water

1 pound cleaned shrimp

1 pound asparagus, hard ends of stems trimmed off

1 pound pasta, cooked and buttered

Grated rind of 2 lemons

1 bunch flat-leaf parsley, chopped

SICILIAN BARBECUE SHRIMP

In New Orleans, barbecue shrimp is not barbecued at all. It never sees a barbecue pit and is served either in the skillet it was cooked in or on a hot plate, along with its buttery sauce for dipping bread. You can serve the shrimp with its sauce in a bowl or over a plate of pasta.

This dish is a classic combination of New Orleans Creole and Sicilian, the original barbecue shrimp created at the restaurant Pascal's Manale. My Nana concocted this version, and she added tomato sauce. But neither the original nor my Nana's was barbecue by any definition.

2 pounds large shell-on shrimp

2 sticks unsalted butter, divided

6 cloves garlic, minced

1 cup Nana's Basic Tomato Sauce (recipe page 20)

½ cup shredded Parmesan cheese

½ cup finely chopped fresh flat-leaf parsley

Dried red pepper flakes to taste

For serving: crusty bread for dipping or cooked pasta

1. Remove the heads from the shrimp and reserve them separately from the unshelled shrimp bodies. Heat 1 stick butter in a large skillet set over medium heat until it begins to foam. Add the shrimp heads and stir until the heads turn bright pink, about 2 to 3 minutes. With a spider, remove them from the pan. You can either discard the cooked heads or reserve them for making seafood stock.

2. Add the garlic to the butter in the skillet. (If you think you need the second stick of butter, add it.) Stir and immediately add the headless shrimp. As you stir, raise the heat as high as it will go. After sautéing 2 minutes, add the tomato sauce and stir until the tomato sauce is hot.

3. Sprinkle the finished dish with the cheese, parsley, and pepper flakes. Serve in shallow bowls with sides of bread or over hot pasta.

SHRIMP AND PASTA SALAD

MAKES 6 TO 8 SERVINGS

This dish is so American, but its success depends entirely on cooking the pasta the way Sicilians do, al dente. (The irony of the importance of this technique is not lost on me.) And even if you cook the pasta correctly, this salad can be mushy if you use a cheap American brand instead of real semolina pasta. Regardless of the brand of pasta, keep in mind that it continues to cook after you drain it.

1. To make the dressing, in a small bowl, mix together the mayonnaise, Parmesan, garlic, and lemon juice. Mash the anchovy and mix it well into the dressing. If the mixture is too stiff, add more lemon juice.

2. Place the remaining ingredients into a large bowl. Pour on the dressing and toss thoroughly. Add salt and pepper, if needed. Remember that the anchovy, the cheese, and the seafood are already salty. Serve immediately.

PASTA SALAD DRESSING

1 cup homemade mayonnaise

½ cup grated Parmesan cheese

2 cloves garlic, minced

Juice of 1 lemon

1 anchovy

2 pounds cooked shrimp, crabmeat, or crawfish tails, or a combination

1 pound pasta, such as farfalle or other forkable pasta, cooked al dente

1 pint cherry tomatoes, cut in half

1 yellow bell pepper, chopped roughly

1 orange bell pepper, chopped roughly

1 bunch Italian parsley, leaves only, coarsely chopped

½ cup roughly chopped fresh basil leaves

Salt and pepper to taste

CRAWFISH PASTA

MAKES 4 SERVINGS

1. Heat the olive oil in a skillet set over medium heat. Add the tomatoes and cook, stirring occasionally, for 5 minutes. Stir in the garlic, then the crawfish tails and the zests. Continue cooking until the crawfish is uniformly heated through.

2. Place the cooked pasta into a large serving bowl and add the basil leaves. Immediately add the crawfish mixture and toss thoroughly. Add salt, pepper, and red pepper flakes. Serve immediately.

3 tablespoons olive oil

4 Roma tomatoes, chopped

5 garlic cloves, sliced

1 pound peeled crawfish tails

Zest of 1 orange

Zest of 1 lemon

1 pound freshly cooked pasta

½ cup chopped fresh basil leaves

Salt and pepper to taste

Red pepper flakes to taste

LINGUINE WITH WHITE ANCHOVIES

MAKES 3 SERVINGS

In Sicily anchovies come in many different forms. You can get them packed in salt, which renders them slightly fermented and akin to a fish sauce from Asia. That version will give you a great umami undertone in tomato sauce. In America it is easier to get anchovies as canned filets or jarred rolled filets. And it is no wonder that many people here don't like anchovies; their anchovy-eating experience is usually limited to desiccated smelly brown strips that lack the complexity of the slightly fermented anchovies typically used as a Sicilian seasoning.

If you can find plump, delicious anchovies in olive oil, that is what you should use for this dish. And if you can ever find fried fresh anchovies on a restaurant menu, order it immediately. Fresh anchovies are wonderful.

Water and salt for boiling pasta

8 ounces linguine

¼ cup olive oil

6 cloves garlic

8 white anchovy fillets

½ tablespoon chili flakes

For serving: 1 cup breadcrumbs; about 10 basil leaves, chopped; ½ cup chopped green Sicilian olives; and your favorite grated cheese

1. Boil a big pot of water with salt and cook the linguine according to package directions. Drain and reserve ½ cup pasta water.

2. Heat the olive oil in a large skillet set over medium-high heat. Chop the garlic and add it to the skillet. Immediately add the anchovies, heat them through, and mash them into the oil. Stir in the chili flakes, the cooked linguine, and the reserved pasta water. Stir well until the sauce thickens.

3. To serve, divide among 3 bowls and top with the breadcrumbs, basil leaves, olives, and grated cheese. Serve warm.

OYSTERS AND PASTA

This dish breaks all the rules about not mixing seafood with cheese. But in New Orleans we have lots of dishes that mix seafood and cheese, so the rule is suspended here. That is a good thing, because seafood and cheese taste good together.

1 pound sturdy pasta, like linguini, just cooked

1 stick butter, cut into 4 or 5 pieces

1 pint fresh oysters, with their liquor

1 bunch parsley, chopped

Zest of 1 lemon

½ cup of grated Parmesan cheese, divided

For serving: freshly ground black pepper and more grated Parmesan

1. Drain the pasta in a colander. Place the butter into the hot, empty pasta pot and let it begin to melt. Return the drained pasta to the pot and toss to distribute the butter.

2. Add the oysters and their liquor, parsley, lemon zest, and half of the cheese. Toss to distribute evenly. By now, the butter should be completely melted. The oyster liquor should combine with the butter and the pasta starches to make a thick sauce.

3. Place everything on a warmed platter and toss on the remaining ¼ cup cheese. Generously grind fresh black pepper over the platter. Serve immediately with more cheese at the table.

TROUT MARINARA

1. Remove all bones from the fish. Place the filets in a bowl and rub sides with the mustard. Set aside in the refrigerator.

2. Pour the oil into a deep skillet and heat over medium-high. The oil is hot enough when a bit of flour tossed in sizzles but doesn't burn. While the oil is heating, in a bowl, whisk together the flour, cornstarch, Creole Italian Seasoning Mix, and salt.

3. When oil is hot, dredge the filets, one at a time, in the flour mixture, coating them on all sides. Set them on a tray. Carefully place 2 filets in the hot oil, being careful not to overcrowd the pan. Cook on one side until golden, about 3 minutes. Turn the filet over and cook on the second side until it's golden, 2–3 minutes. Remove filets and drain on a brown paper bag or paper towels. Repeat until all filets are done.

4. While the fish is frying, heat the Creole Red Gravy. Serve with a spoonful of red gravy over each filet, and garnish with Gremolata. Put any extra red gravy in a sauceboat for the table.

4 large speckled trout filets, or any other mild flaky white fish

1 cup Dijon mustard

Enough neutral oil to fill a skillet 2 inches deep

1 cup all-purpose flour

1 cup cornstarch

1 tablespoon Creole Italian Seasoning Mix (recipe page 23)

2 teaspoons salt

2 cups Creole Red Gravy (recipe page 22)

For serving: Gremolata (recipe page 14)

CREOLE FRITTO MISTO (MIXED FRIED PLATE)

MAKES 6 SERVINGS

Fritto misto is nothing more than an assortment of fried seafood and chicken. I think oysters are particularly delicious when cooked in oil that's been used to first fry chicken livers—it's a wonderful combination.

1. Heat 4 inches oil in a deep pot or fryer oil to 360°F. Combine the cornmeal, flour, Creole Italian Seasoning Mix, and salt and place it in a paper bag. Decide what you will be frying and place it into the paper bag with the flour mixture. Shake the fish or chicken livers (or whatever you're cooking) until it's well coated.

2. Carefully place the fish into the hot oil. Do not overcrowd. Cook until golden brown, about 5 minutes. Remove with a slotted spoon and drain on paper towels.

Enough peanut oil to reach 4 inches in a deep fryer

1 cup fine cornmeal

1 cup all-purpose flour

Creole Italian Seasoning Mix (recipe page 23)

Salt to taste

Oysters

Fish cut into 1½-inch pieces

Shrimp

Squid, cut into pieces

Chicken livers

CHAPTER 7

AT HOME IN NEW ORLEANS
Drinks

Bonu vinu fa bonu sangu. (Good wine makes good blood.)
—Sicilian proverb

After my grandmother, my Papa, and my still-young mother left the crowded family home in Tremé and moved to Lakeview, my Nana had command of her own house. It was a little two-bedroom brick bungalow, typical of others in the neighborhood. I loved that old house, with its ornately carved neo-Victorian furniture. Many of the chairs and the sofa were covered in moss, black, cream, and peach upholstery lined with brass tacks with large decorative heads. The floors were polished oak covered with rugs, and the walls were textured in a cream color and burnt umber. An arched opening separated the living room from the dining room, which was crowded with furniture. Of course, there was a big dining room table with chairs. Along one wall was a large breakfront full of fancy glasses and dishes for Sunday dinner and guests. The drawers of the breakfront held silver and table linens. I loved the starch smell of the drawers and the delicate look of the lace. There was also a sideboard, because there were always too many serving dishes to fit on the table. And there was a record player/radio combination so we could listen to opera records, Dean Martin, Frank Sinatra, baseball games, and radio soap operas.

A swinging door opened to the kitchen. My first memory of the kitchen was of cream-colored, high-gloss plaster walls scored to look like stone. The oil paint had dried hard, and the walls could easily be washed down. A rectangular table was butted against the wall so it could serve as what we would today call a kitchen island, as well as serve as the table. The wooden chairs surrounding the table were simple, their rungs worn from years of rubbing feet. The countertop was black and white ceramic tile that traveled up the wall to form the backsplash. On the wall hung a terrifying plastic black cat, with a clock in its belly, and whose eyes moved back and forth, and a tail that moved like a pendulum.

Before my husband Rick and I could think of marrying, he had to first meet my Nana and pass through her kitchen gauntlet. When anyone visited, including Rick, they had to eat, no matter the time of day or how well she knew them. On Rick's first visit he was required to identify salami and gorgonzola cheese. Nana also informed him that she did not like his moustache and that he was too thin. But since he ate the sausage and cheese with gusto, he passed muster. She could fatten him up later. I had clearly picked an American, like my own father, but by this time I think the family was past that distinction.

Behind the kitchen was a closed-in porch with windows looking out into the backyard. The porch had a glider, which my brother and I loved. In the porch corner was an old freezer where Nana kept her homemade popsicles and huckabucks frozen in paper Dixie cups, just like the ones I had eaten after school from her family's freezer in Tremé.

I'd often answer the back-porch doorbell and would sometimes be greeted by homeless men explaining they were hungry. I'd go tell Nana, and she would say to me, "Tell him to wait on the back steps and I will make a plate." And Nana would assemble whatever there was, heat it, include a glass of beer and dessert, and serve it on a tray. This happened at least once a month, and the hungry strangers were never the same person. I only lived a block away, and no one ever knocked on our back door asking for food. I asked Nana why she so willingly fed these men she didn't know, and she told me she did it because it was Jesus taking a human form and giving her the opportunity to feed him.

Off the porch room was a small laundry room with a washer and dryer, a big, deep sink made out of cement, an ironing board and iron, and a gas burner with a galvanized tin cauldron sitting on it. Inside the cauldron was a long wooden paddle bleached white.

Two bridal wreath bushes in the front yard made beautiful annual displays. Only edible plants grew in the back. My grandparents had no desire to waste precious yard space with landscaping. To them, their yard was a little farm.

Anyone who entered Nana's house typically walked straight to the kitchen. When it was just the two of us, we'd sit at the kitchen table and have coffee and a sesame-seed cookie. In this time before microwaves, Nana would reheat the leftover breakfast coffee by putting the coffee pot in a pan of water on the stove. I would stand on a stool and watch and warn Nana when tiny bubbles began appearing around the edges of the water bath. If I was distracted or if Nana couldn't come quickly enough and the coffee boiled, she would throw it down the drain. Boiled coffee, she explained, was not palatable. We always added warmed milk to leftover coffee, which we didn't drink black because it wasn't freshly brewed. We sugared our coffee, and we'd dunk a cookie into the coffee latte, sharing secrets and planning the day.

SALUTE

On weekends Papa would cut the grass. I would fetch things for him and play while he pushed the lawnmower around the pear trees, the fig trees, the French laurel, and the kitchen garden. I helped sweep the sidewalks, and in the summer heat would get him drinks of water. Papa would wear khaki shorts, an undershirt, and a big work handkerchief (ironed by Nana) either on his head under his straw hat or around his neck. Even though he was Sicilian, my Papa had reddish-brown hair, a red beard, and freckles, and he sunburned easily, so a hat was a must during grass cutting. Sometimes the sun seared so hot that he needed handkerchiefs for both his head and his neck, and he would send me inside to get a second one.

When I'd bring water, sometimes he'd add a shot of scotch from the bottle he hid from my grandmother in the garage. My parents always laughed about this bottle. On grass-cutting days he also drank beer in huge bottles, at least a quart.

Because my parents seemed to approve, I kept Papa's secret from Nana. When the outside chores would be over, he would show me the empty beer bottle.

"How many bottles do you see?" he would ask me.

"One," I would reply solemnly.

"Good," he would say, and he would let me run inside. Nana would ask me, "Did Papa drink beer?"

"Yes," I would answer.

"How many bottles did he drink?"

I would look her straight in the eye and say, "One."

"Only one?" She would ask the question with what seemed a combination of suspicion and relief.

"Only one," I would reassure her. My grandfather would not have asked me to lie for him.

My Nana was not in the least deceitful, so she was easy to deceive. She never asked about the glasses of water I brought out to my grandfather, and I honestly believe it never occurred to her that he kept a bottle of scotch in the garage. I guess I learned the little underhandedness that I know from Papa, and perhaps I should have been appalled. But he knew I would not deceive Nana in any serious way, especially since my parents were co-conspirators in the great scotch and beer coverup.

My grandmother was the most gullible of her family of nine siblings and was always the most easily fooled. All her brothers and sisters enjoyed playing tricks on her. Thankfully she was good-natured about the teasing. But I remember on occasion wanting to protect her; I would be incredulous and almost angry at her for allowing herself to be fooled. Then again, sometimes my parents and I fooled her too. Our favorite joke was to tell her that her food was greasy. That never failed to get her goat.

Even though Nana gave Papa the evil eye if she suspected he drank too much, there was always wine in the house. To Sicilians, wine was food, not alcohol. Wine makes things taste better, and we usually drank it with meals. At family meals children were given a mixture of wine and water. As they got older, the glass would have less water and more wine. By the time a child was fifteen or sixteen, the glass contained only wine. It was not a large glass, and no young person sat around drinking wine. But our schoolmates had to wait to reach the drinking age before they imbibed. By then, we children of Sicilian heritage were fully indoctrinated into the drinking culture.

Heavy drinking in families was almost always limited to weddings and other happy life events, such as baptisms, first communions, etc. And then there were funerals, which were long affairs that included a wake that lasted overnight. In the old days, there was lots of drinking during wakes. I remember my first wake, which was considered an event to spend laughing, crying, talking about the deceased, and drinking. The alcohol at funerals was almost always good, straight liquor, either whiskey, scotch, bourbon, or brandy. Only those who came to pay their respects and then leave drank wine. Some mourners there for the long haul added a bit of water to their glass of whiskey, but no one drank cocktails. The purpose of drinking at a wake was to loosen the spirit as quickly as possible, to mourn better and more completely. Drinking at funerals wasn't about something that was to be tasted and enjoyed.

Other than on these occasions, it was not acceptable to over-imbibe. And that was what I was taught, and that was what I was shown by example. Actually, my mother simply expected that I wouldn't get drunk, because why should I? It was non-Sicilian children who got drunk. Their parents had not allowed them to drink when they were young, and when they were old enough, they didn't know how to handle alcohol. If any of us cousins got drunk, my mother expected us to give each other a talk, and to shun the offender if they couldn't control themselves in the future. Drinking, especially wine, was just a normal thing. You could drink without sneaking it, and there was never a reason to drink too much.

PRESSING ISSUES

My Nana ironed everything. She ironed sheets and pillowcases, her cotton slips, my grandfather's boxers, and even the work handkerchiefs she made from worn-out sheets. To keep everything bright white she boiled clothes in water with bleach in a large cauldron set on a little gas burner in the laundry room. When I was old enough, I was allowed to stand on a chair with a wooden paddle and push the bubbling clothes down into the water. We were cooking those clothes clean. While I stirred the cauldron with the paddle, my grandmother ironed.

Her laundry room seemed to stay damp with steam from the cauldron. It always smelled like chlorine bleach. The air was probably toxic, but we seem to have survived.

Nana's ironing was an elaborate process. After the clothes were washed, those needing starch were soaked in the cauldron, in which Nana had soaked cooked rice. For a fresh scent, she added rose water or lavender to the starch water. Then clothes were added, and we used the trusty paddle to stir everything around. Nana would hand-wring the starched clothes and pile them into a big basket. One by one, she'd pass them through a mechanical wringer that, to me, looked like a big hand-cranked pasta machine. She'd roll the wrung-out clothes and put them into another basket. Only then were they ironed. I loved the transformation the ironed clothes underwent. The damp crumpled masses would emerge dry, crisp, and sweet-smelling.

Unstarched clothes would stand by in another basket, and Nana would eventually hang them outside to dry on the clothesline. When they were dry and invariably stiff, I would shake on rose or lavender water from a bottle with a metal sprinkler top, and they, too, would be transformed into beautifully ironed clothes.

It was my job to put the piles of folded handkerchiefs into their drawers. The small ladies' handkerchiefs went into Nana's top bureau drawer, which was lined with an old pillowcase filled with lavender blossoms and sewn shut. Papa's large, dress linen handkerchiefs went into his bedside table drawer. Work handkerchiefs went into a small chest of drawers in the laundry room, where they could be reached easily from the kitchen or from the backyard.

Nana was not a minimalist. When we finished folding and putting away, she would get her bottle of Coty Straw Hat perfume and put a bit on two work handkerchiefs, one for her and one for me. We worked the rest of the day in a cloud of perfume.

As I got older, Nana allowed me to wield the iron. I began with handkerchiefs and pillowcases and graduated to shirts. It was such a satisfying feeling to turn dirty things into clean, crisp, good-smelling clothes. My mother, too, ironed my father's shirts and many other articles of our clothing. She didn't iron pillowcases and underwear like my grandmother. But she did iron with a bottle of water with a sprinkler top, which we would shake onto already dried clothes.

ALMOND MILK

Long before it was fashionable my Nana made almond milk, usually un-sweetened. If she served a small glass of almond milk after dinner, she sometimes added a tablespoon of sweet Marsala. If you like sweetened almond milk, you can add honey or sugar to taste. You can even soak a vanilla bean or cinnamon stick to perk up the somewhat bland liquid.

1 cup almonds, whole or sliced

2 cups water

3 cups filtered water

Cheesecloth

1. Soak the almonds in the 2 cups of plain water for 24 hours.

2. Drain and place the almonds with the filtered water in a food processor or blender. Puree the mixture until the almonds are finely ground, 3 to 5 minutes. Place several layers of cheesecloth into a strainer and place the strainer over a bowl. Pour the almond puree into the lined strainer and allow to strain until the liquid stops dripping, after about 30 minutes. You might need to move the solids to the side if they get too thick in the strainer. Use the cheesecloth to squeeze out any last bit of liquid, being careful not to let the solids escape into the liquid. Reserve the solids for another use. If the almond milk is too thick, add a bit more filtered water, up to a half a cup.

GINGER MINT TEA

If we needed a pick-me-up during a break from ironing, Nana sometimes made ginger mint tea.

Bring the water to a boil and remove it from the heat. In a teapot or glass jar, add the ginger root and mint leaves, then pour in the hot water and cover with a lid. Wait 20 minutes, then pour the brewed tea into a teacup. Add sugar and a slice of lemon, if desired. This tea can also be served chilled.

1 quart water

1 piece ginger root, about 1 inch long, chopped into 10 pieces

1 cup mint leaves

For serving: sugar and lemon slices

COFFEE

Fresh coffee is best drunk black. If you reheat coffee, I suggest doing so by the cup in the microwave, an option that wasn't available to my Nana. You can salvage the flavor by adding hot milk. To make a cappuccino, steam and froth milk with a frother, and add it to hot coffee.

Dark-roast coffee, espresso grind

Sugar

Lemon peel

Fill the bottom chamber of a 2-ounce moka (a stovetop espresso pot) with water. Add coffee to the coffee basket insert and tamp down the grounds with a spoon. Place the insert into the pot. Screw on the top of the pot and place the entire pot on a burner. Boil at high heat and promptly remove from the heat when you hear a gurgling noise, when the brewed coffee has been forced into the top of the chamber of the pot and the bottom chamber is almost empty. Pour the coffee into a small cup. Add sugar, if desired. Twist the strip of lemon peel over the cup, as you would over a cocktail, and let the oils flavor the coffee. Serve immediately.

ICED COFFEE PUNCH

MAKES 12 SERVINGS

Coffee with chicory is delicious in this recipe. You can use cold coffee, but you'll have a harder time dissolving the sugar.

In a large covered container, mix together all the ingredients except the ice, stirring well to dissolve the sugar. Refrigerate the sweetened coffee a few hours. When ready to serve, pour the cooled coffee mixture into a punch bowl and add the ice. Ladle into punch cups.

4 cups strong brewed coffee, cooled to barely warm

1 cup brandy or rum

1 cup whole milk

1 cup half-and-half

½ cup sugar

Grated zests of 1 lemon and 1 orange

4 cups ice cubes

BITTERS

My Nana and the entire New Orleans Sicilian community drank *aperitivos* and *digestivos,* which are important ingredients in today's craft cocktails. Nana bought her *amari,* bitter liqueurs, at Solari's. She also concocted liqueurs she did not intend to be consumed in cocktails. These special liqueurs were her cures for upset stomach, for overeating, and for a lax appetite due to illness. Even though you could use it in cocktails, she drank the bitters from this recipe medicinally. (Even the famous Peychaud's bitters was originally medicinal.)

You can customize this recipe by using lemon peel instead of orange peel, crushed rosemary leaves instead of gentian root, and caraway seeds or star anise instead of anise seeds. You can also add cardamom seeds, allspice, and cinnamon quills.

½ cup dried orange peel

6 Indian cloves

1 teaspoon gentian root

1 tablespoon anise seeds

2 cups (151-proof) grain alcohol

¼ cup sugar

1. Mix the orange peel and spices in a large jar and cover with the alcohol. Cover the jar and let sit 3 to 4 weeks, shaking the jar every day.

2. Decant (strain) out the orange and spice solids and reserve both the solids and the liquid. Tie the solids in several layers of cheesecloth and mash them with a heavy bottle to break them up. Over high heat, place 3 cups water in a pot with the mashed solids in the cheesecloth. When the liquid reaches a simmer remove from heat, cover the pot, and allow to steep at room temperature 4 or 5 days.

3. Strain the infused mixture through clean cheesecloth and discard the solids. In a clean bottle, mix the spice infusion with the reserved infused alcohol and the sugar and shake well. Cover the bottle and store at room temperature. This recipe is potent, so use these bitters by the dropper.

COFFEE AND CREAM LIQUEUR

Nana made her own liqueurs. She simply did not trust things made by someone else; she felt it would not be made with her level of care. This recipe was her substitute for hot coffee following dinner in the summer. After the dishes were done, she and my Papa would sit on the porch with paper fans on a stick, fanning themselves and sipping coffee and cream liqueur. It was their precursor to today's iced coffee.

1½ cups extra-strong espresso or cold-brewed coffee

1 cup sugar

1 vanilla bean

2 cups half-and-half

1½ cups 100-proof vodka

1. In a saucepan mix together the espresso, the sugar, and the vanilla bean. Heat until the sugar is dissolved. Add the half-and-half, bring to a simmer, and immediately remove from heat.

2. Take out the vanilla bean and strain the mixture into a bowl. Stir in the vodka. Pour into a sterilized jar, leaving 2 inches headroom. Cover and store in the freezer at least a week before serving. Serve frozen in a glass, where it will melt into a delicious liqueur.

CITRUS LIQUEUR

MAKES 8 CUPS

Someone in the neighborhood had prolific kumquat trees, and one day they gave my grandmother several brown paper grocery bags full of ripe fruit. Thus, Citrus Liqueur was born. When Nana had lots of jars of liqueur, she would give it as a hostess or birthday gift. When giving as a gift, she would put at least one kumquat in the bottle for an interesting presentation. She saved bottles just for these situations.

1 pint fresh kumquats

1 fifth 100 proof bourbon

3 cloves

3½ cups Simple Syrup (recipe page 135 or purchased)

1. Rinse the kumquats well and place them in a large jar. Cover the kumquats with the entire bottle of bourbon. Cover the jar and allow to sit 60 days out of the sunlight.

2. Remove and drain the fruit and save them for another use. Add the cloves, cover the jar, and wait another week.

3. Remove the cloves. (Don't leave the cloves in the bourbon more than a week, or the clove flavor will dominate.) Pour the alcohol through a fine sieve into a clean jar. Add the Simple Syrup and stir. For a clearer liqueur, strain it through a coffee filter. Bottle in sterilized jars and keep in the freezer. Serve cold.

LIMONCELLO

MAKES 8 CUPS

This is the classic liqueur that would have been made with the peels of the many lemons that grew in Sicily, which were the same lemons Sicilians in New Orleans imported and distributed around America. These were the same lemons that came in through the Port of New Orleans during the burgeoning canning industry and were turned into citric acid for the industry. These were also the lemons that spurred both Florida and California to establish lemon orchards to rival those of Sicily. In time, domestic lemons grew successfully enough to stem to the importation of Sicilian lemons.

New Orleans has lots of satsuma oranges, and you can use their peels in this recipe to make an excellent liqueur too. Some Sicilians add anise seeds to the macerated mixture, but most Americans do not enjoy that flavor.

10 organic lemons

1 fifth vodka

3 cups filtered water

2½ cups sugar

1. Wash the lemons to remove dirt and residue and dry them. Remove the zest with a vegetable peeler, taking care to make the peel as thin as possible to avoid cutting into the bitter pith. The peeled lemons can be saved for another use.

2. Place the peels into a 2-quart glass jar. Pour the vodka into the jar and cover with a lid. Store at room temperature out of direct sunlight for 7 days.

3. Heat the water in a pot. When it begins to simmer, add the sugar. When the sugar begins to dissolve, remove from heat and stir to dissolve any remaining sugar crystals. Allow to cool. When the syrup reaches room temperature, pour it into the jar of peels and vodka and cover. Let the mixture steep at room temperature 24 hours. Strain the mixture and either discard the peels or keep them for another use.

4. Fill sterilized bottles with the limoncello and cap them. Allow limoncello to age at least 2 weeks in a dark cabinet at room temperature. Then store in the freezer. Serve extremely cold in shot glasses.

SPARKLING LIMONCELLO

Although she was easily fooled, Nana was keenly intelligent about flavors, and she used what was available with great imagination. Sparkling Limoncello was her invention. It's always refreshing and is festive for a party.

Cold limoncello

Cold prosecco

For serving: twists of lemon peel

Place 1 tablespoon limoncello in a sparkling wine flute. Fill the glass with cold prosecco. Garnish with a twist of lemon peel and serve immediately.

NECTAR SYRUP

This is our family version of the famous New Orleans pink, almond-flavored soda fountain syrup. Just as Herbsaint and Peychaud bitters make you think of New Orleans wherever you are, nectar syrup can bring back those memories too. Today, nectar syrup is most commonly used to flavor snoballs, but it is really great in cocktails. Substitute nectar syrup for grenadine in any drink, or even instead of simple syrup. It also deliciously moistens a slice of pound cake.

3½ cups sugar

2 cups water

2 tablespoons almond extract

1 tablespoon vanilla extract

¼ cup grenadine syrup

Place the sugar and water in a pot and heat to a simmer. Cook until the sugar is dissolved and remove from the heat. When the mixture is cool, add the extracts. Then add the grenadine. Place in a capped sterilized bottle and keep in the refrigerator.

MINT SYRUP

MAKES 1 CUP

This recipe can be adapted to use just about any herb—thyme, chamomile, and ginger all make delicious syrups. Simply substitute your favorite herb for the mint.

1 cup hot Simple Syrup (recipe follows)

2 cups fresh mint leaves

2 strips of lemon zest

In a saucepan, bring the Simple Syrup to a boil and remove it from the heat. Place the chopped mint leaves and lemon zest into the pot. Steep 3 to 4 hours. Strain out the solids, pour the syrup into a sterilized jar, and store in the refrigerator. Keeps in the refrigerator 6 weeks.

SIMPLE SYRUP

MAKES ABOUT 1½ CUPS

Combine the sugar and boiling water in a large jar. Cover and shake until the sugar is completely dissolved. Cool and store in the refrigerator up to 1 month.

2 cups sugar

2 cups boiling water

ROSEMARY WATER (FOR LAUNDRY)

MAKES 1 QUART

Nana bought rose water and lavender water to make the laundry smell good, but she also made a heavenly rosemary water to use on my Papa's clothes because she thought it smelled more masculine. Originally, she did what everyone else did with laundry waters—she used a bottle with a metal sprinkle top. In later years she used a spray bottle. If her rosemary water turned too dark for spraying on white cloth, she diluted it with more water. But on plaids or colored clothing, she'd use the dark water at full strength.

1 quart boiling water

5–6 sprigs fresh rosemary

Pour the boiling water and rosemary into a covered glass jar. Let it sit 2 hours, then remove the rosemary.

CHAPTER 8

BECOMING NEW ORLEANIANS
Meat and Poultry

Sicilians build things like they will live forever and eat like they will die tomorrow.
—Attributed to Plato

Like Italians living throughout the United States, Sicilians who moved to New Orleans cooked more and more meat, instead of mostly vegetables and pasta as they had in Sicily. The primary reason for this change in diet was that in Italy, beef, fowl, and seafood had been associated with wealth, whereas produce and grains were for the peasantry. In Sicily eating meat once a week was considered abundance. Those who only ate meat on feast days, which was probably offal or cured meat made from trimmings and waste, typically associated it with feasting.

In early twentieth-century New Orleans, meat was inexpensive, abundant, and available. In particular, Louisiana's cattle industry was robust, so beef was relatively inexpensive and plentiful. In comparison to its cost and availability in Sicily, beef seemed extremely accessible to the new immigrants.

Regularly serving something once out of reach was part of the reason Sicilians had left their home country, so despite their new home's overt prejudice, difficulty adapting to new cultural norms, and language problems, these immigrants felt they were living up to the American promise by eating meat. Forget today's Mediterranean diet, with its emphasis on fruits, vegetables, and grains. New Orleans's large Sicilian population wanted to be marked as successful and generous to guests, and serving meat was a mark of assimilation and wealth. Thus, the pasta course transformed into something that included a huge portion of protein, as opposed to using meat as a flavoring. This idea would flabbergast an actual Italian.

NANA'S BRUCCIALUNA

When I was a child, I did not understand the enormity of the world. I had no comprehension of the fear and anxiety my Nana must have faced when she made the decision to sail to New Orleans from Sicily. And living my comfortable middle-class American life, I did not grasp the desperation, the hunger, or the loss that must have been experienced by all those who left Sicily to make a new home in America. I did know that the island called Sicily was far away, but that was all. It didn't matter to me that Nana had had to endure untold hardships in her native homeland, because in my childish way the fact that she was here now for me was enough.

In the 1950s and 1960s, when there were still pockets of close-knit Sicilian families in New Orleans who spoke the Sicilian dialect, I didn't learn that language because my mother and father spoke English with each other. Today, when I hear Sicilian it reminds me of the warmth of family and belonging. As with that language, those long-ago times gave me a set of comfort foods that are firmly fixed in my taste memories. I remember those daily doses of raw garlic, and the act of grating Parmesan cheese and the fragrant release of its aroma. I remember olive oil with everything, and artichokes and eggplant, black olives and pistachios. These things were always at the ready when it was time to pull out food for an unexpected visitor. When it was time for dinner, a litany of slow-cooked meals and dishes are forever embedded in my mind. *Bruccialuna* is one of the dishes, both because I was allowed to participate in making it, and also because it was so pretty on the plate. Wrapped in that roll of beef are all of the family memories—tastes, language, and love.

At large gatherings in New Orleans we may serve gumbo, jambalaya, or even red beans and rice, but with my family it was *bruccialuna,* a rolled steak, the cut and size depending on the number of guests. The meat was stuffed with boiled eggs, colorful vegetables, and a cheese and breadcrumb mixture that make an artistic presentation with each slice. I remember the kitchen chair with a step stool that my Nana kept by the counter just for me to stand on as we cooked. When we made *bruccialuna* she would butterfly a beef roast and pound it between two pieces of wax paper. I was then allowed to use an empty wine bottle or sometimes a wooden rolling pin to pound it even thinner. My Nana would finish the job to ensure that the thickness of the meat was consistent throughout.

As in kitchens everywhere, as we cooked, my Nana transmitted her stories to me. Of course, I was learning to cook, but in my recollection these times were opportunities to learn her story, to learn life's lessons, and to talk about other things.

I would closely observe her habits. The routine of saving coffee grounds and eggshells to fertilize the garden—long before anyone was using the word "composting" in common speech—made me subconsciously aware of the circle of the food cycle. Making stock from food scraps wasn't frugal to me—it was just what was done. I wasn't trying to avoid waste; I was just following her routine.

To the breadcrumbs for the *bruccialuna,* Nana would add grated Parmesan cheese, dried oregano, and garlic powder, and I was allowed to use a big wooden spoon to combine the ingredients. She would add enough eggs to make a good paste. I was then allowed to pat the breadcrumb mixture onto the flattened meat. After that we became artistic.

When rolling up the meat we had to keep aesthetics in mind; the roll would be sliced for serving, so the cross-section had to look really appealing on the plate and on the platter. This meant arranging hard-boiled eggs, strips of carrots and strips of cheese, and sometimes basil or spinach leaves in a manner that would make an attractive presentation after the *bruccialuna* was sliced. After rolling the meat tightly and tying it in several places with string, Nana seasoned the outside with salt and pepper. In order to form a nice crust on the outside, she would brown the meat roll in olive oil in a heavy pot. After it was well browned, she would set the meat aside for the next step.

Bruccialuna traditionally calls for a deeply flavored sauce to balance the beefy flavor. To intensify the flavor of her basic sauce, for *bruccialuna* Nana would add a bit more olive oil and melt an anchovy or two in the pot she had used to brown the meat and scrape up the goodness of the fond stuck to the bottom. She would then add two tablespoons of tomato paste and allow that to caramelize with the anchovies and the fond. Then she would add chopped onions, a bit of celery, a grated carrot, the zest of half of a lemon, and the zest of an orange. (Most of these elements were already in her tomato sauce, but intensity was important for the *bruccialuna*.) Only then would she add the deep-red sauce.

After the sauce came to a simmer, she would add the browned *bruccialuna,* which would disappear under the tomato sauce. As the dish cooked down and grew thicker, the *bruccialuna* would become visible. When she had the time, she would put the pot in the oven and let the meat and the tomato barely simmer in the oven, the flavors becoming ever more intense. But sometimes she just cooked it on top of the stove.

Pasta was always served with this traditional beef roll. Nana would center the finished beef on her big, round, white platter rimmed with gold. My Nana gave that platter to me, and now my son uses it. When she was serving the dish, she would toss the pasta with a bit of the sauce and place the pasta in a circle around the roll. Then she would slice it and put the remaining sauce in a bowl with a ladle. She garnished the dish with more lemon zest, grated Parmesan cheese, and freshly chopped parsley. This dish was usually greatly anticipated and was eaten—at least at first—in silence, simply because it was so good.

My immediate family loved eating at Nana's. And those satisfying times were and are captured in memories that bubble to the surface when family members use her plates and platters, and we smell the aromas of her Sicilian kitchen and traditional dishes like *bruccialuna.*

A long time ago this dish was a regular item on New Orleans restaurant menus, but it is something almost impossible to order these days. Why don't Creole Italian restaurants serve *bruccialuna* anymore? Maybe this dish fell out of favor because it is more complicated to make than the often delicious but quick pasta sauces that can be prepared quickly. Or maybe it's because, just like the Creolized food of New Orleans, which is a social invention created collectively in homes, Sicilian food is considered *la cucina casereccia,* home cooking, and not special enough for a restaurant. Even though early Creole Italian restaurants served what was eaten in homes, today most of them do not; they're chef driven.

Sadly, many people also no longer make *bruccialuna* at home, so younger generations have no idea what it is. Although there are still many of us who recall a pot of *bruccialuna* simmering on their grandmothers' stoves, lots of younger people of Sicilian heritage are removed from this experience, as they are from many other labor-intensive dishes, and from those big family dinners. Like the complicated modern turducken, a whole turkey stuffed with graduating smaller sizes of various poultry, *bruccialuna* is something to eat for a feast. Turducken is easy to find in meat markets already assembled because it's *en vogue.* But if you long for *bruccialuna* but don't want to make it yourself, unfortunately, you'll have a hard time finding a New Orleans grocer or restaurant chef who shares that nostalgia.

NANA'S BRUCCIALUNA

MAKES 4–6 SERVINGS

BRUCCIALUNA STUFFING

Mix the breadcrumbs, grated cheeses, garlic, and oregano in a bowl. In a small bowl, beat one raw egg with a fork. Add the beaten egg to the cheese mixture and season with salt and pepper. If the consistency seems dry, mix in the second egg in the same manner. Set aside the stuffing, hard-boiled eggs, carrots, and strips of cheese.

½ cup Seasoned Breadcrumbs (recipe page 101 or purchased)

½ cup grated Parmesan cheese

½ cup grated provolone cheese

3 cloves garlic, minced

2 tablespoons dried oregano

1 or 2 raw eggs

Salt and pepper

2 hard-boiled eggs, peeled

2 long carrots, scraped and cut in half lengthwise

8 to 10 strips of mozzarella cheese, cut from slices

THE MEAT

1. Place the flank steak or the butterflied roast between 2 sheets of plastic wrap or wax paper and beat it into an even thickness with a meat mallet or an empty wine bottle. (Do not beat it to the point that it begins to break, only to about ½ inch.) It is important that the meat be of an even, consistent thickness. Salt and pepper the meat. Heat the olive oil over medium-high in a large oven-safe pot or Dutch oven.

2. Evenly spread the prepared breadcrumb mixture over the meat. Center the 2 hard-boiled eggs side by side on the edge of a long side of the meat and lay 2 carrot halves and the cheese strips down each long side of the meat.

3. From the long end with the eggs, carrots, and cheese, begin rolling the meat jelly-roll fashion. When about halfway rolled, tuck in anything that wants to slip out of the roll.

4. Use kitchen twine to tie the roll snugly. Brown the tied meat roll in the hot oil, about 4 to 6 minutes on all sides. Remove from the pan, reserving the oil in the pan. Set both the meat and the uncleaned pan aside.

1½ pounds beef flank steak, or a small butterflied beef roast

Salt and pepper

2 tablespoons olive oil

BRUCCIALUNA SAUCE

1. To make the sauce, reheat the oil in the pan you used to brown the meat. Dissolve the anchovy in the hot oil, stirring up the bits of browned meat from the bottom of the pan. Add the tomato paste and caramelize 3 to 5 minutes. Add the onion and garlic and cook until translucent, about 7 minutes. Add the celery, carrot, and zests. Continue cooking another 5 minutes.

2. Preheat your oven to 325°F. Add the tomato sauce and wine to the vegetables in the pot and stir well and cook until the sauce simmers. Carefully drop in the *bruccialuna,* along with any juices that have accumulated on the plate. Simmer 10 minutes.

3. Cover the pot and place it in the oven. After 30 minutes, turn the beef roll to expose the cooked side. Continue baking, covered, an additional hour. Remove the cover from the pot and cook another 30 minutes.

4. To serve, toss the pasta with sauce to cover lightly and place it on a platter. Place the beef roll on top of the pasta and sprinkle with cheese, parsley, and lemon zest. Serve immediately.

1 anchovy filet

2 tablespoons tomato paste

1 onion, finely chopped

3 cloves garlic, minced

2 stalks celery, finely chopped

1 carrot, grated

Grated zest of one lemon

Grated zest of one orange

2 cups tomato sauce (Homemade is best, such as Nana's Basic Tomato Sauce; recipe page 20)

1 cup red wine

For serving: hot, cooked pasta, grated Parmesan cheese, and freshly chopped parsley and lemon zest.

MEATBALLS

Meatballs, now ubiquitous in America and found in some form all over Eurasia, are known in Italy as *polpette* (*polpetta* is the singular). *Polpette* can be made from any minced meat. In Italy, they are no larger than a walnut and are usually either eaten alone or in a soup. Italy has no dish equivalent to our spaghetti and gigantic meatballs, although some tourist restaurants serve it because Americans request it.

In Italy, where famine and poverty caused so many Sicilians to come to America, meat as the central part of the meal is not the norm. Indeed, when a *polpetta* is served alone on the plate, it is often for a celebration or other special meal. To convert that meatball into something served with mounds of sauce-covered pasta and covered in cheese is American. It's sort of a shame that spaghetti and meatballs, along with pizza, have come to represent the contributions of Italy to the cuisine of America. The roots of these dishes are there, but the details have been transformed into something totally American, and they are particularly embraced in the Gulf South.

In New Orleans, every Italian restaurant wants to be considered authentic, but at the same time they serve the unauthentic dishes we have come to expect. For example, pasta with meatballs has been served at Pascal's Manale for more than one hundred years. Pascal Radosta's wife, Francesca, and her sister used to roll the meatballs and make the red gravy for the restaurant at their house up the street on Louisiana Avenue, and the younger generation working in the restaurant would get the call to pick it up. Francesca's recipe is still used today. But as delicious and seemingly traditional as the Manale recipe is, the dish's roots are Creole Sicilian, not Italian. (A side note: When Pascal's Manale introduced barbecued shrimp, the women in the Radosta family would wash, iron, and fold the cotton shrimp bibs Pascal Radosta handed out with the peel-and-eat dish.)

Italian restaurants along the Gulf Coast are known for offering meatballs and spaghetti, the dish a perfect example of the transformation of ethnic cuisine into American cuisine. This beloved dish is a grand illustration of the underlying American idea that more is more. For example, we in New Orleans, as in the rest of the nation, tend to treat pasta as a vehicle for a large volume of sauce. Until recently we haven't understood that when it comes to Italian food, the pasta itself, in one shape or another, should be the star. Sauce should pair with the pasta, but it should never drown it. The high chance of sauce overwhelming pasta's flavor is why, in many modern American restaurants and home kitchens, the best pasta is often presented simply with olive oil and a bare sprinkling of cheese. And really good American-Italian restaurants, even those that serve too much sauce on their pasta, are serving pasta al dente. It took Americans time to learn, but most now know that mushy pasta tastes no better than canned meatballs and spaghetti, and that's a travesty.

When it comes to saucing meatballs, the New Orleans roux-enhanced Creole red gravy so many cooks around here serve is robust and often sweet with sugar. When done right, the sweetness is the perfect foil for the saltiness of the cheese and the umami of the meatballs and tomato. Since traditional American sauce is made with canned tomatoes, some form of brightness beyond sugar is needed for balance. That extra zing can be achieved by the addition of wine vinegar, lemon juice, orange zest, hot pepper, or some other secret ingredient closely guarded by the chef, such as the carrots my Nana always tossed in. Restaurants and home cooks have made reputations on the balance of their tomato sauce.

MEATBALLS

MAKES 20 SMALL OR 10 LARGE MEATBALLS

1. Preheat your oven to 325°F. In a large bowl, mix the beef and the pork together thoroughly with your hands. Try to do this with economical movements so the meat won't toughen. Mix in the breadcrumbs and seasoning mix or salt and pepper.

2. In a separate small bowl, mix the milk and egg together with a fork. Pour the milk mixture into the bowl of meat and mix thoroughly. The mixture will be wet. If it seems too dry, add a bit more milk.

3. Oven method, for dropping into a tomato sauce: To prevent sticking, coat your hands with olive oil and form the meatballs the size of golf balls. Spread the 3 tablespoons olive oil on a baking sheet and place the meatballs on the sheet, making sure to leave a bit of space between each. Bake 30 minutes. You can place these straight from the oven into a simmering sauce.

4. Stovetop method, for serving without a sauce: Roll the meatballs to the desired size and place them on a baking sheet. Cover with plastic wrap and chill at least 30 minutes. Remove from the refrigerator and heat olive oil over low heat in a skillet. Cook, being careful not to crowd the meatballs, and don't move them around too much; you don't want them to fall apart. Cook, until you have a nice brown crust on each meatball, turning halfway through, for a total of about 20 minutes.

1 pound ground beef

1 pound ground pork

1 cup Seasoned Breadcrumbs (recipe page 101 or purchased)

Creole Italian Seasoning Mix (recipe page 23) or salt and pepper to taste

½ cup milk

1 large egg

3 tablespoons olive oil, plus more for coating your hands

FENNEL SAUSAGE

MAKES 1 POUND, OR 8 SMALL PATTIES

This makes a delicious breakfast sausage patty, which works with great with eggs. You can sauté the sausage loose and toss it over pasta, or mix it with breadcrumbs for a more substantial meat stuffing. You can also shape the mixture into large patties to make Italian hamburgers.

My favorite time to eat fennel sausage was at Nana's house on Saturday nights, when my little brother and I often stayed when my parents went out. My Nana would often quickly put this easy-to-cook sausage together and serve it with broccoli or baked tomatoes.

1 pound ground pork, about 25 percent fat

1 teaspoon ground fennel seeds

1 teaspoon salt

1½ teaspoons Creole Italian Seasoning Mix (recipe page 23)

1 or 2 tablespoons sweet Marsala wine

1 tablespoon bacon fat

1. In a large bowl, mix together the ground pork, fennel seeds, salt, and Creole Italian Seasoning Mix. Add 1 tablespoon wine. If the mixture seems too dry, add the second tablespoon of wine.

2. Make 8 small patties and place them on parchment paper on a cookie sheet. Heat a tablespoon of bacon fat in a skillet and fry the patties until they are brown on both sides until done.

SAUSAGE AND PEPPERS

MAKES 4 SERVINGS

Like tomatoes, bell peppers originated in the Americas. The non-green peppers in particular found their way into the food of Sicily. The irony of them returning across the Atlantic to America is worth noting.

1. Over a medium-high flame, heat the olive oil in a large skillet. Cook the sausages on all sides until thoroughly cooked, about 8 minutes. Remove from the skillet and keep them warm. Add the sliced onions and cook until soft and beginning to caramelize, about 10 minutes. Add the sliced peppers and cook 10 minutes more, stirring and tossing the vegetables so that they cook evenly.

2. Add the garlic and the Creole Italian Seasoning Mix. Cook another 2 minutes. Return the sausages back to the skillet and cook until they are heated through thoroughly. Serve over polenta and top with Parmesan cheese.

¼ cup olive oil

4 sweet Italian sausages

1 yellow onion, sliced

½ green bell pepper, sliced

1 red bell pepper, sliced

1 yellow bell pepper, sliced

1 orange bell pepper, sliced

5 cloves garlic, minced

Creole Italian Seasoning Mix to taste (recipe page 23)

For serving: hot, cooked polenta and grated Parmesan cheese

ITALIAN SAUSAGE MAQUE CHOUX

MAKES 4–6 SERVINGS

Stretching a bit of meat with a lot of vegetables is a very Sicilian way to eat. Using traditional Louisiana maque choux as a base and making it a full meal with the addition of sausage changes the flavor of the sausage, of course, but it also takes advantage of fresh corn and peppers in season. To stretch this dish even more, add a chopped fresh tomato.

1. Heat the fat in a large skillet over high heat. When the oil is hot, add the raw fennel sausage and sauté until the sausage is cooked, about 6 minutes. Break up the meat as you cook so it stays loose and does not form clumps or patties.

2. Add the corn and cook, stirring several times, for 1 minute. Add the onion and sauté 30 seconds. Add the garlic, salt, and the Aleppo and black peppers and cook 1 minute. Stir in the cream, bell pepper, and scallions and simmer until heated through, about 2 minutes. Remove from the heat. Spoon over warm grits and dust with more Aleppo pepper. Serve immediately.

2 tablespoons bacon fat

1 recipe Fennel Sausage (recipe page 144)

1½ cups fresh corn scraped from the cob (about 2 ears)

1 medium onion, chopped

1 clove garlic, minced

1 teaspoon salt

1 teaspoon Aleppo pepper, plus more for garnish

½ teaspoon freshly ground black pepper

⅔ cup heavy cream

⅓ cup minced red bell pepper

⅓ cup thinly sliced green onions (scallions)

For serving: hot, cooked grits

STUFFED MIRLITONS

This dish takes advantage of the native squash known outside New Orleans as chayote. New Orleanians typically eat mirlitons stuffed, but it is also delicious thinly sliced and tossed raw into a salad, or even sliced into eighths and pickled. The flavor of the squash is mild, so it picks up the flavor of the stuffing. If you really want to jazz up your mirlitons, after they come out of the oven top them with a spoonful of tomato sauce.

2 large mirlitons

Olive oil

Salt and pepper

1 pound Italian sausage

2 cups Seasoned Breadcrumbs (recipe page 101 or purchased)

½ cup grated Parmesan cheese

1. Preheat your oven to 325°F. Cut each mirliton into 2 pieces through the stem end. Use a melon baller to pull the seed out of the halves. (Some cooks boil their mirlitons. But since this is really a tender and crispy squash that tastes like nothing after it is boiled, I skip the boiling step.) Brush the 4 mirliton halves inside and out with olive oil and sprinkle the halves with salt and pepper.

2. Mix the Italian sausage with the breadcrumbs. Place ¼ of the mixture into each mirliton half, using all of the stuffing mixture. It is okay if the hole from the seed is too small to hold much, just pile everything over the entire cut surface of the mirliton. Place the stuffed mirlitons in a casserole or baking dish. Top with Parmesan cheese and bake 90 minutes. Serve warm.

VEAL PARMESAN

MAKES 4 SERVINGS

1. Preheat your oven to 475°F. Place the flour into a shallow bowl and season it with salt and pepper. Break the eggs into another bowl and beat them and the lemon zest with a fork. Place the breadcrumbs into a third bowl.

2. Season the veal with salt and pepper. Working with one cutlet at a time, dredge in the seasoned flour, making sure to cover both sides. Dip each dredged cutlet into the egg mixture, then in the breadcrumbs, covering both sides. Place breaded cutlets on a platter or tray.

3. Heat about 5 tablespoons of oil at a time in a skillet over medium heat. Sauté the cutlets without overcrowding until the crumbs are golden, about 3–4 minutes per side. Add oil as needed. Place the cooked cutlets on a baking sheet or an ovenproof serving platter. Spoon about ¼ cup sauce over each cutlet; top with 1 slice provolone, and sprinkle with 1½ table-spoons Parmesan cheese. Bake until cheese is golden and bubbly, 4–5 minutes. Garnish with parsley.

½ cup all-purpose flour

Salt and pepper to taste

4 eggs

Zest of 1 lemon

1½ cups Seasoned Breadcrumbs (recipe page 101 or purchased)

8 small veal cutlets, pounded ⅛ inch thick

½ cup olive oil

2 cups Nana's Basic Tomato Sauce (recipe page 20)

8 slices provolone cheese

¾ cup grated Parmesan cheese

For serving: 2 tablespoons roughly chopped parsley

SCALOPPINI

1. In a shallow dish mix together the flour, salt, pepper, and Creole Italian Seasoning Mix. Dredge the scaloppini on both sides. Add the oil to a large skillet set over medium heat. When the skillet is hot, add the dredged scaloppini. Do not crowd them. Allow them to brown quickly, about 5 minutes, and then brown on the other side up to 4 minutes. Remove from the pan.

2. In the same skillet, over high heat sauté the mushrooms, shallots, and garlic until all the mushroom liquid evaporates. Add the wine and broth and deglaze the pan. When the liquid is at a brisk simmer, add the minced capers and lemons and simmer until slightly thickened, 5–10 minutes.

3. Add the scaloppini and heat through. Remove to a heated platter and top the meat with the mushrooms and sauce. Sprinkle generously with chopped parsley. Serve with lots of good bread for dipping into the sauce.

½ cup all-purpose flour

Salt and pepper to taste

Creole Italian Seasoning Mix to taste (recipe page 23)

6 scaloppini (veal, pork, turkey, or even grilled eggplant slices)

3 tablespoons olive oil

2 cups sliced cremini mushrooms

1 shallot, finely chopped

3 cloves garlic, minced

1 cup white wine

1 cup chicken broth

¼ cup capers, minced

1 whole lemon, thinly sliced

For serving: ½ cup chopped fresh parsley and Italian bread

CREOLE SHRIMP, CHICKEN, AND ITALIAN SAUSAGE

MAKES 6 SERVINGS

This dish is a Creole Italian version of a *bolito misto* (mixed boiled dish). It reads more complicated than it is—it's actually a really simple dish to put together. I usually serve it over grits instead of the typical Creole way of serving gravy dishes over rice.

1. For sausage, preheat oven to 350° (or use a stovetop grill pan). Place the red gravy and bay leaves in a large saucepan and turn the stove flame on medium-low. When sauce comes to a simmer, add the chicken thighs and cover. Let the chicken cook while you prepare the sausage. If at any time the sauce gets too thick and sticks, stir in ¼ of the wine.

2. While the chicken is simmering, bake the sausages in the hot oven or on a grill pan until they are cooked through, 30 minutes. Add them and their juices to the sauce in the pot. Stir, then cover, and cook 25 more minutes. By the end of this cooking time the chicken should have cooked one hour. Don't forget to check if the sauce is sticking or if it's too thick. If so, stir in more wine.

3. With the sauce at a simmer, add the shrimp. Stir, cover, and cook 10 more minutes. Be careful not to overcook the shrimp. Serve hot over grits and top with grated Parmesan cheese at the table. (If you serve it over rice, omit the cheese.)

6 cups Creole Red Gravy (recipe page 22)

2 bay leaves

3 boneless chicken thighs, each cut in two

3 links sweet Italian sausage, each cut in two

1 cup red wine, if needed to reduce sticking

½ pound raw, peeled shrimp

For serving: hot, cooked grits and grated Parmesan cheese

CREOLE COQ AU VIN

I really don't have many family recipes for chicken. Most Sicilians in New Orleans considered chicken filler, as something to stretch a shrimp dish, for example.

1. Chop the bacon into small strips about ½ inch wide. Fry slowly in a heavy pan to render the fat and crisp the bacon. Remove the bacon and reserve, and leave the fat in the pan.

2. Season the flour with the salt and pepper and dredge the chicken pieces in the seasoned flour. Brown the chicken pieces on all sides in the rendered bacon fat. Remove the chicken and set it aside.

3. In the same pan, sauté the onions, mushrooms, carrots, and garlic. Add the bourbon and carefully light it on fire. When the flame dies out, add the wine, broth, bay leaves, Creole seasoning, and 1 teaspoon thyme. Cover and simmer at least an hour. Uncover and taste and correct the seasoning.

4. Make a gremolata by mincing together the parsley, lemon zest, and remaining ½ teaspoon dried thyme. Arrange the chicken over a bed of hot grits and sprinkle with the gremolata. Serve warm.

6 slices bacon

½ cup all-purpose flour

Salt and pepper to taste

1 chicken, cut into 6 pieces

2 cups pearl onions

2 cups sliced mushrooms

2 carrots, cut into coins

2 cloves garlic, chopped

¼ cup bourbon

1 bottle dry red wine

2 cups chicken broth

3 bay leaves

2 teaspoons Creole seasoning

1 teaspoon dried thyme, plus an additional ½ teaspoon

¼ cup chopped fresh parsley

1 tablespoon grated lemon zest

For serving: hot cooked grits

FRIED CATFISH

MAKES 6 SERVINGS

This recipe is in this chapter because our family considered catfish the same thing as meat. Unlike today's farmed, mildly flavored catfish, the catfish of my childhood was strictly wild-caught, and it had a strong, muddy flavor. We never baked or stuffed our catfish, as did the Creoles and Cajuns; we fried it like a scallopini and served it like meat, sometimes with pasta and usually topped with tomato sauce (which was like our Italian ketchup).

2 pounds catfish filets

1 cup Dijon mustard

1 cup all-purpose flour

1 cup cornmeal

1 tablespoon Creole Italian Seasoning Mix (recipe page 23)

2 teaspoons salt

Enough vegetable oil to fill a skillet 2 inches deep

For serving: lemon wedges

1. Slice the filets thinly. Place them in a large bowl and use your hands to thoroughly coat each piece with mustard. Cover and refrigerate.

2. In a shallow bowl mix the flour, cornmeal, Creole Italian Seasoning Mix, and salt. Whisk until well blended. Begin heating the oil.

3. While the oil is heating, one at a time dredge the filets on all sides with the flour and cornmeal mixture and set them on a tray. The oil is hot enough when a bit of the flour mixture dropped in sizzles but doesn't burn. Carefully add a few filets without overcrowding. Fry on one side until golden, about 3 minutes. Turn the filets over and cook on the second side until golden, 2–3 minutes. Remove filets and drain on a brown paper bag or paper towels. Repeat until all filets are done. Serve warm with lemon wedges.

CHAPTER 9

HERE AND NOW
Desserts

Lettu di Duminicani, tavulu di Cappuccini, lussu di Binittini. (The Dominicans for a bed,
the Capuchins for food, and the Benedictines for luxury.)
—Old Sicilian proverb

When I was a child and my grandmother and mother were immersing me in the New Orleans Sicilian realm, it was already a fading world. The original generation of immigrants was aging, and the first generation of Sicilian Americans were a large step removed from the motherland. My mother, first-generation American, was able to easily maneuver in the city without the overt prejudice her mother had experienced. My mother spoke English like a native because she was one, yet she was still a Baiamonte. But she married a non-Sicilian with the decidedly American name of Cleve Williams, and thus, as a Williams, I operated seamlessly in and out of the two worlds.

Unlike my mother, I didn't speak the Sicilian language. As a second-generation American I had lost that link between language and land. The only reason my mother spoke Sicilian was because that was the language of her home. My father didn't know Sicilian; he only spoke English. This meant that my mother and grandparents spoke to him in English, so English was the language of our home. Even so, when my grandparents and my mother spoke with each other in Italian, I could understand a lot of the dialect.

By the time my little brother was old enough to remember things, English was the only language spoken at gatherings of our extended Sicilian side of the family. Although my grandparents were still alive then, many members of their generation and the older generation were gone. None of my "once-removed" cousins spoke Sicilian. Even among the older generations, only my mother, who was a first-generation American, still spoke Sicilian.

And make no mistake, the Italian language has little in common with Sicilian. When my mother made her first pilgrimage to Italy, she learned the hard way that she didn't speak Italian; she was treated disparagingly for speaking Sicilian. My entire extended family seemed to accept that my generation, my cousins, my brother, and I, would not be expected to speak Italian, only to understand a few phrases. But I still had food as a connection to those ascendant generations. And I had the experience of knowing people, my family, who had actually lived in and come of age in Sicily.

So, is this the loss of the Sicilian language terrible? Not really. The Sicilian-speaking community in New Orleans has shrunk immensely, but the Sicilian American diaspora endures, and the vestiges of our culture live on in photographs, memories, and, especially, food. Speaking several languages might be good for your brain, but it's not necessary to thrive.

ARE WE OF ITALIAN DESCENT?

This is probably a question that makes no sense to an actual Italian. Italy has been unified long enough so that Sicily is not separate anymore. The movement of Risorgimento (resurgence) that began taking hold in the nineteenth century happened at the same time the seeds of the Civil War in America were fomenting. Although unification was not complete, Italy convened its first Parliament in 1861. By the time the U.S. Emancipation Proclamation freed enslaved Africans and their descendants in 1863, and especially when our Civil War ended in 1865, the newly united Italians were

seeing the economic effects of unification, which were not all positive.

Many had a hard time adjusting to being Italian, instead of identifying with one of the regional states. That's why those from Sicily who came to New Orleans considered themselves Sicilians, and not yet Italians. Even by the latter part of the nineteenth century and into the twentieth century, those areas of Italy that felt disempowered were still not embracing their place in unified Italy. They still tied their primary identity with their region, thus so many people in New Orleans still consider themselves of Sicilian descent and only technically Italian.

During one of my visits to Sicily it was clear to me that Italy is still a country of regions, and that people still identify deeply with their regions. That is definitely true in Sicily, where the regional language is still spoken, Sicilian songs are still sung, and after all these years the food and history are still part of the pre-unification identity.

The roots of the Italian food eaten in New Orleans can be seen on the Island of Sicily. For example, the muffuletta bread much loved in New Orleans is still sold in the Sicilian bakeries and still known by the name muffuletta. That loaf would be recognized by any New Orleanian. Recently, Italian food historian Alberto Capatti visited New Orleans to eat muffuletta sandwiches, as a way to compare the Sicily of today with historical Sicily. He saw the Italian food of America as food trapped in time. He saw it as dishes that were once eaten in Italy, but that are no longer eaten there, although they are still eaten here. The muffuletta was one example. The bread is still eaten in Sicily, but not the sandwich. This finding surely doesn't surprise me. Most of the mass immigration at the turn of the twentieth century came from a single location, and because of immigrant attitudes and expectations, the uniform Sicilian influence on New Orleans cuisine was extremely intense.

FADING IDENTITY

Without the "old people" (I add quotation marks because I am now an old person) to beat the drum over this distinction between Italy and Sicily, more and more New Orleanians describe themselves as being of Italian descent first, not Sicilian. My children are third-generation Americans, and to them they are just Americans. They love some of the Sicilian dishes I make, but they have never experienced the childhood family memories of a living a culture different than America's. They have no personal associations with other ethnicities. They abstractly realize they have various ethnic backgrounds, including Sicilian, but that understanding is purely academic.

For longer than a century, so many Sicilian-influenced things have become Creolized and Americanized. As those of us of Sicilian heritage have become American, we look nostalgically back on what was. But what we often forget is that what we think of as Italian or Sicilian is probably something nostalgic for the Italians and Sicilians actually living in Italy. Today, life in

Italy and in Sicily is not what we were told about the Old Country. Italy is a modern European country. It is not fossilized in the nineteenth and early twentieth centuries.

I have to admit, I was disappointed when my kids grew old enough to embrace the traditions of being Sicilian and they didn't. It made me think back to my mother's disappointment when I only chose certain traditions to adopt. But I do understand that, when my children rejected anise-flavored, sesame seed–crusted biscotti, they, unlike me, had not grown up eating sugared anise seed, shipped over from relatives in Sicily. My exposure to this at an early age is what made me love anise flavor. As my grandmother aged and the relations in Sicily died, we stopped getting those care packages. My mother did not feed sugared anise seed to my children, and neither did I. This lack of connection is why my children didn't embrace the flavor. We had not laid the foundation for eating anise as my grandmother so thoughtfully had.

Fortunately, I have vivid memories of making anise cookies with my grandmother, as well as of all our cooking adventures. And I want to continue this tradition of Sicilian cooking with my granddaughters. We don't even have to bake cookies together, just cook. (But baking cookies is always fun.)

BISCOTTI REGINA (ITALIAN SEED COOKIES)

MAKES 3 TO 4 DOZEN

This was Nana's recipe. She made it without a mixer and relied on feel. The exact ingredient proportions changed with the weather. When Nana, and later my mother, were both too arthritic to knead the dough, I would do it, which gave me the chance to learn the proper feel. These cookies are hard enough to stand up to dunking, but they are not very sweet. They do, however, go well with sweet wine.

My grandmother was a snob about sesame-seed cookies, and she considered hers the best. Brocato's Bakery cookies, I was told, were not hard enough, thus they broke when dipped in wine. They also tasted much milder. Nana had not adapted her recipe for American palates as had Brocato's, so hers had much more anise oil. Today, Brocato's cookies seem devoid of anise, all because so many Sicilian Americans have lost their taste for that flavoring.

Even though my mother loved these biscotti as much as I did, she didn't make them herself until Nana died. After that my mother and I made them every year at Christmas, using pounds and pounds of flour and butter. Today I make biscotti when I am feeling nostalgic. They remain for me a bridge to the past and a constant reminder of St. Joseph altars. Having never met my Nana, my own children are not enamored of these biscotti. Perhaps the cookies are not as wonderful as I recall, when they are objectively judged. That is of little importance.

3½ cups all-purpose flour

2 teaspoons baking powder

⅛ teaspoon salt

1 cup (2 sticks) unsalted butter

¾ cup sugar

1 large egg

2 teaspoons anise extract or oil

1 teaspoon pure vanilla extract

½ cup milk

1½ cups sesame seeds

1. Preheat your oven to 350°F. Lightly grease a couple of large baking sheets. In a large bowl, combine the flour, baking powder, and salt. In the bowl of a standing mixture with a paddle attachment, cream together the butter and sugar until light and fluffy. Beat in the egg, anise, and vanilla.

2. Gradually add the flour mixture to the butter mixture. Beat on medium speed until dough is soft and smooth, about 4 minutes.

3. Place the milk into a shallow bowl. Place the sesame seeds into another shallow dish. Form a piece of dough into a ball the size of a large softball. Knead the dough ball on a hard, clean surface. If the dough is sticky, butter your hands.

4. Roll the dough into a long log about 1 inch in diameter. Cut the log into 2-inch pieces. Dip each piece into the milk and then into the seeds, entirely covering the cookie. Place the seeded cookies on the prepared cookie sheets and bake until the bottoms are lightly brown, 17–20 minutes. Cool on wire racks and store in an airtight container at room temperature.

BENNE BISCOTTI (SESAME-SEED COOKIES)

MAKES 3 TO 4 DOZEN COOKIES

This is the classic version of Italian seed cookies. It calls for less butter and more egg than Nana's recipe, which changes the texture and makes the cookies even more sturdy and able to stand up to dipping in wine, milk, or cappuccino.

1. Preheat your oven to 350°F. Sift the flour, baking powder and salt together. Add the sugar to the dry ingredients, then work in the butter with your hands.

2. Add the eggs and continue working the dough until it all comes together. Stir in the milk a little at a time, until you have a firm dough. (Don't add too much milk, or the dough will be sticky, especially on a humid day.) Roll the dough into snakes about ¾ inches in diameter. Cut into 2-inch-long pieces. Dip the pieces into the remaining milk, then dredge in sesame seeds.

3. Place the cookies on an ungreased cookie sheet and press each down slightly. Bake until lightly brown and very, very crisp, 12 to 17 minutes. Remove from cookie sheet and cool thoroughly before placing in an airtight container. They keep for months.

3 cups sifted all-purpose flour

2 teaspoons baking powder

½ teaspoon salt

½ cup sugar

¾ cup (1½ sticks) room-temperature butter

2 eggs

Grated rind of one lemon

1 tablespoon anise oil, or almond oil if you are not a fan of anise

½ cup milk

½ pound untoasted sesame seeds

BOURBON BALLS

This is another one of those frugal dishes made from a method and not a recipe. When I need to salvage hard, stale brownies, I crumble them in my hands into a bowl. I add bourbon, just enough to make the crumbs stick together, but not too wet. I then form the mixture into balls. That's it!

Depending on my mood and how the brownies react, I sometimes roll the balls in powdered sugar or ground pecans. If I have leftover blondies, I use the same method to make rum balls rolled in ground pecans.

You can keep bits and pieces of stale brownies in a freezer bag, until you have enough to make these bourbon balls. They'll look newly made, not like leftovers. And they're particularly attractive served in pleated paper cups.

CANNOLI

When I was a young adult, one day I went to one of the Gendusa's bakeries to buy cannoli. I needed a nostalgia fix, but I wasn't a regular at this bakery. I asked for a dozen cannoli and the man behind the counter smiled at me and asked me my name. I told him, and he pressed further, asking me for my Italian name. I shared my mother's name and those of my grandparents. I asked how he knew I would have an Italian name connected to me. He told me that I had asked for a dozen cannoli. Americans ask for a dozen cannolis. He then explained that people who grew up only hearing Italian use the plural correctly, even when they are unaware of doing it. He found it a subtle way to identify people of Italian heritage, and he gave me a thirteenth cannolo for free.

When I was very young and shopped with my Nana, we often made our way to Brocato's on Ursulines for cannoli. We would buy half a dozen. I loved looking at all the beautiful trays of cookies and pastries, but I was not allowed anything but cannoli. (My Nana didn't make cannoli.)

CANNOLI SHELLS

1. In a large bowl, mix together the flour, sugar, and salt. Add the butter and use your hands to work it into the flour mixture until everything feels like sand. Work quickly because the heat from your hands will begin to melt the butter.

2. To the sandy mixture blend in the wine and egg yolk until it forms a dough. As thin as possible, flatten the dough into a circle. Wrap the dough circle in plastic wrap and put it in the refrigerator.

2 cups all-purpose flour

¼ cup sugar

¼ teaspoon salt

2 tablespoons unsalted butter, cut into small cubes and frozen

½ cup dry white wine

1 egg yolk, beaten

CANNOLI FILLING

1. In a large bowl, whip together the ricotta and powdered sugar. In a jar, add the cinnamon, allspice, and cloves. Cover and shake well. Add the spice mixture to the ricotta and blend to mix well.

2. In a separate bowl whip the cream with the vanilla until stiff. Gently fold the whipped cream into the ricotta mixture. Stir in the chocolate chips and lemon zest. Refrigerate while you fry the shells.

FRYING THE CANNOLI

You'll need cylindrical forms to shape the cannoli shells. Metal cannoli forms are widely available, but many a broomstick has been cut into 4- or 5-inch lengths to use as forms. Or you can buy a wooden dowel from the hardware store and cut it to lengths you like.

If you do not want to make traditional cannoli shells, it is easy to cheat and make a large pizzella (recipe follows) and bend it and cool it around a dowel about the width of a broom handle. Then fill as you would a cannolo shell. You can even make them from chocolate pizzella dough.

1. Heat the oil in a large pot to 360°F. Meanwhile, take the cannoli shell dough out of the refrigerator. On a lightly floured board, roll pieces of dough into 4-inch rounds to about ⅛ inch thick. You should have about 24 rounds. Take each circle of dough and wrap it around a cannoli form. Glue the seams together with a dab of beaten egg. Be sure it is secure on the form. Stretch the edges of the dough at the open ends slightly up from the form so oil can get between the form and the dough.

2 cups whole-milk ricotta

½ cup powdered sugar

1 teaspoon ground cinnamon

⅛ teaspoon ground allspice

⅛ teaspoon ground cloves

¼ cup heavy cream

½ teaspoon vanilla

¼ cup mini semisweet chocolate chips

Zest of one lemon

1 quart peanut oil or canola oil (or any neutral oil)

Flour to dust the rolling surface

1 large egg, beaten

¼ cup chopped pistachios or pecans

Powdered sugar for dusting

2. Use tongs to carefully lower each dough-covered form into the heated oil. Do not drop them in. Fry until golden, about 3 minutes. Remove the shells from the oil and use a clean towel to help slide the cannoli off their forms. Allow them to drain on a paper towel and cool.

3. Use a pastry bag to squeeze the filling into the shells. If you do not have a pastry bag, use a Ziploc bag and cut one of the corners. Fill from both sides and let the filling meet in the middle. Dip each end in the chopped pistachios. You can also use chocolate chips on one side and nuts on the other. Dust the finished cannoli with powdered sugar.

PIZZELLE

MAKES 14–18 LARGE WAFFLE COOKIES, OR ABOUT
3 DOZEN SMALLER COOKIES

1. Heat a pizzelle maker according to manufacturer's instructions. While the iron is heating up, whisk together the flour and baking powder in a bowl. Break the eggs into a separate bowl and whisk them together. Add the sugar and continue whisking until well combined. Stir the egg mixture into the dry ingredients. Mix in the oil and extract.

2. When batter is a uniform color, drop from a teaspoon into the center of the heated iron. (This will result in a cookie about 3 inches wide. If you want larger cookies, say for making an ice-cream cone, use a rounded table-spoon.) Close the iron and cook until golden, between 30 and 45 seconds. If your electric iron has a light on it, the light will cue you when it's time to open the cover. Remove the cookies from the press and let them cool on a wire rack. (They crisp as they cool.)

1¼ cups flour

¾ teaspoon baking powder

3 large eggs

½ cup sugar

¼ cup olive oil

2 teaspoons vanilla or almond extract

PIZZELLE VARIATIONS

- I made this recipe with vanilla, because anise is not terribly popular. If you use half vanilla and half anise extract, you'll have a more traditionally flavored cookie.

- To make a chocolate cookie, substitute ½ cup of flour with ½ cup of unsweetened cocoa. And by using ½ teaspoon of vanilla dough and ½ teaspoon of chocolate dough side by side, you can make a chocolate and vanilla cookie.

- If you are making cheating cannoli, wrap warm pizzelles around the handle of a wooden broom and allow them to cool. When they are crisp, stuff them with the traditional ricotta filling and garnish the edges with chopped pistachios. Why should you feel guilty for cheating?

- If you make small pizzelle you can make cookie sandwiches by spreading the cookies with Nutella or almond butter and jam, or the ricotta cannoli filling. Top the filled cookie with another cookie. Your sweet sandwich cookie is limited only by your imagination.

CASSATA SICILIANA (RICOTTA CAKE)

MAKES 8 SERVINGS

This pillowy cake is filled with chocolate-studded ricotta and enrobed in marzipan that's glazed and decorated with candied fruit. It's another dish that was likely influenced by the Arabs who ruled Sicily for a time. If you do not have a cassata pan, use any 9-inch pan, preferably with flared sides. Most Sicilian cakes, like this one, are prepared according to specific instructions, and are dense and elaborate. The quick-fix, boxed-type airy cakes we know in America are not part of the Sicilian kitchen.

This dessert was always available at celebrations when I was a child, but as I grew older, I saw it less and less frequently. It is not something you can toss together in a jiffy, so you have to be prepared to devote the time to it. Probably the long time it takes to make cassata has contributed to its decline in popularity. That's a shame, because it is stunning, both visually and in taste, and it's history in a pan.

CASSATA FILLING

1. Dust a rolling pin with powdered sugar and roll out the marzipan in a circle large enough to line the bottom and sides of a 9-inch cassata or baking pan. (Traditionally the marzipan would have been colored green.) Transfer the marzipan to the cassata pan and press it against the sides and bottom.

2. Melt the chocolate and paint it all over the marzipan in the pan, making sure to hide all the marzipan. Allow the chocolate to set. Meanwhile, place the ½ pound powdered sugar, ricotta, candied fruit, chocolate chips, vanilla, and lemon zest into a bowl and mix well. Set aside in the refrigerator. Bring to room temperature before spreading on the sponge cake or it will tear the cake.

½ pound powdered sugar, plus more for dusting

5 ounces marzipan

4 ounces dark chocolate, melted

1 pound ricotta

½ cup chopped candied fruit

3 ounces mini chocolate chips

¼ cup vanilla

Zest of one lemon

CASSATA SPONGE CAKE

1. Preheat your oven to 340°F. Thoroughly coat an 8-inch round cake pan with a cooking oil spray with flour. Use an electric mixer on medium-high speed to cream together the eggs and sugar until the mixture is light yellow and fluffy, about 7–10 minutes. Beat in the vanilla and salt.

2. Sift the flour into the bowl, stopping about 3 times to fold it into the egg mixture. Pour the batter into the prepared pan. Don't smooth the top and don't bang the pan on the counter. It will even itself out in the oven.

3. Bake 40 minutes. Turn off the oven and leave it slightly ajar. Leave the pan inside the oven 10 minutes, then remove it from the oven and cool in the pan 10 minutes. Run a knife around the edge of the pan to loosen the cake. Remove it from the pan and cool thoroughly on a wire rack.

4. Slice the cake into 2 even horizontal layers. Place one cake slice in the bottom of the cassata pan lined with marzipan and chocolate. Brush or spoon half the Marsala over the cake layer. Top that layer with the room-temperature ricotta mixture, spreading it evenly. Top the ricotta with the remaining layer of sponge cake, and brush or spoon on the remaining Marsala.

4 large eggs, at room temperature

½ cup sugar

1 teaspoon vanilla

⅛ teaspoon salt

Zest of one lemon

1 cup cake flour

4 tablespoons sweet Marsala wine

CASSATA CAKE GLAZE AND ASSEMBLY

Slowly whisk the sugar into the egg white, whisking until a glaze is formed. Turn the assembled cake out onto a rack. Pour the glaze over the marzipan. Refrigerate the cake at least an hour. When ready to serve, decorate with candied fruit.

½–¾ cup powdered sugar

1 egg white

Decoration: candied fruit

LEMON PECAN CORNMEAL CAKE

MAKES 8 SERVINGS

Because this cake is better if made the day before, it is perfect for entertaining. If I have kumquats that have been sitting around in brandy or other spirits, I drain them well, coarsely grind them, and add them to the top of the cake about 10 minutes before the cake is done. When I remove the springform ring, the top of the cake is decorated with kumquats that reflect the cake's citrus flavor. This dessert is delicious without this little addition, and my trick helps use those up those kumquats, which cannot be wasted.

1. Preheat your oven to 325°F and set a rack in the middle. Oil a 9-inch springform pan. In a small bowl, sour the milk by stirring it together with the lemon juice. Set aside until needed.

2. Place the pecans, cornmeal, sugar, and lemon zest into the bowl of a food processor. Pulse until the nuts have formed a fine meal and the dry ingredients are thoroughly integrated. Add the baking powder, baking soda, and salt. Pulse once or twice.

3. Transfer the meal to a large bowl. Stir in the soured milk, eggs, oil, and vanilla until everything is well incorporated.

4. Spoon the batter into the prepared pan and place the pan on a cookie sheet to avoid accidents in your oven. Bake until the center springs back when lightly touched, 50 to 55 minutes. Cool completely in the pan, and then release. This cake is best when cured at room temperature 24 hours. Store under a cake dome or wrap in cling wrap. Sprinkle with powdered sugar before serving.

½ cup milk

Juice and zest of 1 lemon

1½ cups pecans pieces

1 cup stone ground yellow cornmeal

¾ cups sugar

1½ teaspoons baking powder

½ teaspoon baking soda

½ teaspoon salt

3 large eggs, beaten

¾ cup olive oil

1 teaspoon vanilla extract

For serving: powdered sugar

GRANITA

Granita is a fine alternative to sorbet when you do not have an ice-cream maker. It is just as delicious, but with a coarser, yet fluffier texture. Instead of using fruit, you can make granita with coffee or just lemon juice, both of which are traditional. If you make this substitution, use 4½ cups of coffee or juice instead of fruit, and freeze and scrape as described.

1. Place all ingredients in a food processor or blender and process until smooth. Pour the liquid into a metal pan. A 9×13-inch pan is a good size. Place the pan into the freezer. After 30 to 45 minutes scrape the freezing mixture with a fork. This creates the right texture for the granita. Place the pan back into the freezer for another 30 minutes.

2. Repeat 2 or 3 more times. Different fruits freeze differently, so you will have to make your own decisions. The goal is to have tiny crystals piled into a serving dish.

3. After the last fluffing and scraping with the fork, freeze 2 hours before serving. Fluff the frozen mixture before serving and divide into serving bowls or champagne coupes. Garnish each serving with a drizzle of good balsamic vinegar or lemon zest.

4 cups (1½ pounds) fresh, soft fruit

¼ cup lemon juice or wine (If you use sweet wine, be careful about adding sugar.)

¼ cup sugar, depending on the sweetness of the fruit and the liquid

A pinch of nutmeg or cinnamon, or your favorite spice

For serving: balsamic vinegar or lemon zest

HUCKABUCKS

These are the frozen homemade popsicles that my Nana and her sisters made at their house in Tremé, and which Nana continued to keep on hand at her home in Lakeview. I was fairly old before I bought a popsicle from an ice-cream truck, since there were outstanding ones at my Nana's house and there was no waiting.

There are so many things you can use to make these frozen treats. The healthiest version is probably fruit juice. We made them with Kool-Aid or Flavor-Aid, and many other neighborhood kids made them with Coca-Cola and root beer. Variations on this simple recipe abound. Consider using evaporated milk mixed with fruit juice. You can also freeze a banana and yogurt smoothie this same way.

Our method: Line up small Dixie cups on a jelly roll pan, fill them ¾ full, and place them on a shelf in the freezer. After about 30 minutes place wooden ice cream spoons or reused popsicle sticks upright in the freezing liquid in the cups. Huckabucks are best after spending the night in the freezer.

We had two methods of eating them, either by using the spoon to scoop up the melting liquid, or by peeling off the paper cup and holding the treat by its handle and licking and biting into it.

LEMON ICE

MAKES 6 SERVINGS

Since the New Orleans summer is so long and hot, it lends itself to desserts that cool you.

2–2½ cups Simple Syrup (recipe page 135 or purchased)

2 cups lemon juice, freshly squeezed

Grated zest of 2 lemons

Combine all ingredients and stir well. Pour through a sieve and chill in the refrigerator at least 2 hours. Pour the mixture into the canister of an ice-cream maker and freeze according to manufacturer's directions. Spoon it into an airtight container and freeze about 30 minutes before serving.

FIG ICE CREAM

1. Preheat oven to 400°F. Halve or quarter the figs, depending on their size. Toss in a bowl with the cane syrup, cinnamon, and cloves. Spread the prepared figs on a cookie sheet lined with parchment paper and bake 30 minutes. Remove from oven and allow to cool.

2. While the figs are roasting, make the ice-cream custard. Place sugar and yolks in a medium bowl and whisk until fluffy, about 5 minutes. In a sauce-pan set over medium heat, stir together the milk and cream. When the mixture is almost boiling, slowly add ½ cup of the milk mixture into the egg mixture and mix well. Add the egg mixture to the remaining milk in the pan and cook over low heat, stirring constantly, until the mixture thickens, 2–3 minutes. Strain if desired. Stir in the vanilla and allow to chill thoroughly.

3. Take the cooled figs and chop roughly in a food processor. Stir together the chopped figs and the vodka and set aside. (Vodka keeps ice cream from becoming hard and crystallized.) Place the chilled custard into an ice-cream maker and freeze according to manufacturer's directions. Ten minutes before the cycle is finished, add the figs and finish freezing the ice cream. Place the ice cream in a covered freezer container and freeze at least 4 hours before serving.

1 pound fresh figs

2 tablespoons cane syrup

¼ teaspoon ground cinnamon

⅛ teaspoon ground cloves

¾ cup sugar

6 egg yolks

2½ cups whole milk

1½ cups heavy cream

1 teaspoon vanilla extract

2 tablespoons vodka

Sea salt

BRANDIED KUMQUATS

MAKES EIGHT 8-OUNCE JARS

This recipe is not sweet, and the aged kumquats are delicious when added to a sauce for roasted chicken or in cakes that call for citrus. After you've eaten the last kumquat, the remaining liquid makes a wicked Old Fashioned cocktail.

2 quarts kumquats

6 cups brandy

2 tablespoons whole cloves

1. Wash kumquats and make sure any tiny stems are removed. Score a small "x" on the stem end of each kumquat and drop them into sterilized glass jars. (I use 8-ounce canning jars, but you can use jars of any size.) If you have kumquats leftover, try to force them into one jar or another.

2. Heat the brandy to a simmer. While waiting for the brandy to heat, place one clove in each jar. Add additional cloves sparingly. Use a ladle to fill each jar with the heated brandy and screw on the lids. Allow the covered jars to sit at least 6 weeks in a dark cabinet.

JAPANESE PLUM (LOQUAT) JAM

MAKES 8 PINTS

The Japanese plum (loquat) is a familiar fruit in Sicily, where it is called *nespola* (plural being *nespole*). The New Orleans corruption of this word is *mispoli*. My Nana considered these small, deep gold, oval fruits a delicious free treat, because in New Orleans so many trees were on public land, where unharvested fruit would drop and rot. We collected *nespole* and made a delicious jam out of the fruit we didn't eat.

So many people in New Orleans have these trees, and it is a shame to not use the fruit. As children, my friends and I would often climb the trees and stuff ourselves, having spitting contests with the large, slippery, copper-colored seeds. I have heard people say they don't cook Japanese plums because of the trouble it takes to remove their seeds. Actually the seeds are easy to pull out when the fruit is cut in half. This seems like a lame excuse to waste such deliciousness. The taste is as delicate as apricot, and halves can be dried like plum tomatoes for later eating. I was never good at waiting, though. I always wanted to eat them right away.

1 gallon of loquat fruit

5–6 cups granulated sugar, depending on the fruit's sweetness

12 whole lemons, chopped (including peels)

Cardamom seeds

1. Wash and seed the loquats. Place the prepared fruit in a large glass, stainless steel, or other nonreactive bowl. Sprinkle the sugar over the fruit and toss to cover entirely. Cover with plastic wrap and allow to sit at room temperature overnight.

2. Place the sugared fruit and its juice into a large jam pot. Stir in the lemons, being careful not to tear up the loquats. Cook at a simmer until the mixture thickens and coats a spoon, about 45 minutes. Occasionally remove the scum that forms. (Keep the scum, which transforms into a wonderful syrup after it melts. This process takes a few hours, but it is worth the wait. You can't beat this syrup when poured into sparkling wine, a sort of loquat bellini.)

3. Ladle the hot jam into jars. Add one cardamom seed to each jar. Process the jars in a hot water bath according to the manufacturer's directions. If you use pint jars, you will need 8 jars.

APPENDIX

A Creole Italian Pantry

To avoid a special trip to the market, keep the following items on hand to create Creole Italian dishes.

IN YOUR REFRIGERATOR

Anchovies

Artichokes

Bread

Broccoli

Butter

Capers

Cauliflower

Celery

Cheeses—various, including rinds

Cream

Eggplant

Eggs

Fennel

Figs, both dried and fresh

Garlic

Lemons

Milk

Olives, cured

Onions

Oranges and other citrus

Pancetta

Peppers

Radicchio

Rennet

Salume, various

Yeast

Zucchini

PANTRY ITEMS

Almonds

Anchovies

Apricots, dried

Chickpea flour

Chickpeas

Coffee

Cornmeal

Fava beans

Flour, all-purpose, unbleached

Lentils

Mushrooms, dried

Olive oil, extra-virgin

Pasta, dried

Pecans

Pine nuts

Polenta or grits

Rice

Risotto

Semolina flour

Sesame seeds

Sugar

Vanilla

Vinegars—balsamic, wine, cane, others

Walnuts

THE BAR

Amaretto

Amari

Anise-flavored liqueur, such as Herbsaint

Brandy or cognac

Fernet-Branca

Liqueurs, various

Marsala, sweet and dry

Prosecco

Vermouths—sweet and dry, white and red

Vodka or grain alcohol for making liqueurs

Wines—various white and red

HERBS AND SPICES

Almond oil or extract

Anise oil

Anise seeds

Basil

Bay Leaves

Fennel seeds

Nutmeg

Oregano

Parsley, flat leaf

Peppercorns

Red pepper flakes

Rosemary

Sage

Salt

Thyme

Vanilla

SPECIAL EQUIPMENT

Cheesecloth

Colander

Food processor

Frother

Ice-cream maker

Immersion blender

Mezzaluna

Microplane grater

Moka (Espresso pot)

Parchment paper

Pasta machine

Pasta roller

Pastry brush

Pizzelle iron

Springform pan

Stand mixer

String

INDEX OF RECIPES